GOD'S WORD FOR THIS WORLD

GOD'S WORD FOR THIS WORLD

BISHOP THOMAS JOHNSON, SR.

J Merrill Publishing, Inc.
434 Hillpine Drive
Columbus, OH 43207
www.JMerrill.pub

Library of Congress Control Number: 2021924314
ISBN-13: 978-1-954414-41-9 (Paperback)
ISBN-13: 978-1-954414-40-2 (eBook)

Book Title: God's Word For This World
Author: Bishop Thomas Johnson, Sr.

To my wife, Ellazean, and my children, who have so graciously shared me with the world.

CONTENTS

PART III

PART I

1

IT'S TIME TO MOVE OUT OF HERE

MY INHERITANCE IS WAITING FOR ME

Exodus 12:1-24, Psalms 30:5, Psalms 118:24, Hebrews 11:1, John 15:19, Psalms 24:1, II Chronicles 20:20, I Corinthians 2:9, Numbers 23:19

Jesus, who knew no sin, died on Calvary's cross for sin to redeem man back to God. For this reason, you can't give up in the middle of the test. You owe him *too* much.

The church has become like a social club, an elite society battling a syndrome called *"entitlement."* As a result, countless churches are out of touch with the community. They don't understand what others are going through, which is quite unfortunate.

Many Christians are messed up, and they sing praises to God one moment and then are popping pills the next. It's time out for being hypocritical. Try God, prove him - hold him at his word; he cannot lie. (Numbers 23:19)

Whatever you're in, is God not greater? The bible states he'll deliver you out of it all. (Psalms 34:19) Stop thinking like a loser if you have plans on winning; there's an inheritance waiting on you. Stop reliving your past. Concentrate on your new beginning in God. Don't spend this year bound, stressing about material wants but redirect your attention to your *"purpose."* Ask yourself, *"What would make me happy?"* It's time to move out of this place and get your inheritance. Blow the devil's mind and praise God where you are, even in your worst state. Get up. It's time to move!

2

MAGNIFY THE LORD
FOCUS

*II Kings 6:1-16, II Corinthians 5:17, Matthew 6:33, Hebrews 11:1,
II Timothy 3:1-7, Isaiah 53:1, Philippians 4:19, Hosea 4:6, Psalms 103:2,
Psalms 27:3-5, Romans 5:8, Ephesians 2:19, James 4:8*

Unfortunately, there are people in the world who don't care who they hurt as long as they get what they want. Jesus loves you so much that he left a life of privilege to live less privileged. Everyone needs a magnifying glass. Magnifying glasses are designed to make small things appear larger. And every Christians's toolbox needs a magnifying glass as well as a mirror. Whatever you place most attention on throughout the year, that's what you magnify. But the God I serve is greater than this. Change your focus for this year. Fear will stop you from having the victory you desire and what God intends for your life. What you focus on will determine your day. Look at the bigger picture.

Don't try to resist the devil without praising God in the process. You've got to see yourself out before you get out. It doesn't take long for God to change your position. It can happen just like that. So, look in the mirror and change yourself - major thinking.

3

CHURCH, STOP PLAYING

Exodus 32:6, Ezekiel 37:1, Galatians 5:16, Jeremiah 3:15 & 33:4,
Isaiah 55:8 & 45:7, I Peter 3:7, Philippians 2:5, Deuteronomy 7:6,
Romans 8:1, Ephesians 5:25

A number of churchgoers are unprepared and playing church. Many attend service out of routine, neglecting the importance of worship, fellowship, and salvation. As a result, they fail to take God and church seriously, but it's time for the church to excel.

Children of God should display attributes of the father and have his word in their hearts. God has given you pastors after his own heart to teach the knowledge and ways of the Lord. **(Jeremiah 3:15)** Jesus is the head of the church, and the church is the bride of Christ.

God loves man with agape love, unconditional love for his creation. God looks at your potential - *what you can be* despite your faults and flaws. Nevertheless, this society is driven by sex and the spirit of lasciviousness, envy, and jealousy. People are not striving to be like God today. Yet, they use popular "church clichés," insinuating Christ with no substance behind it. As a result, a growing generation does not know God or His Spirit, resulting in an increasing number of politicians legalizing same-sex marriages and other abominable legislation that appears right in their sight.

God is not concerned with what the world is doing. He's interested in what you *(the church)* are doing because you carry his name. So many are constipated in their spirits, having "respect of person" and not valuing your relationship with the Father. Time is up for the disobedience and foolishness of the past. Life is too short to be careless with your faith. God has sent his warning, church, stop playing!

4

THE DILIGENT SHALL BEAR RULE

*Proverbs 4:23 & 12:24, Proverbs 22:29 & 21:5, Psalms 34:10,
Hebrews 11:6 & 12:1, Isaiah 53:5, I Thessalonians 5:5*

God is challenging believers to seek his face, *"but they that seek the Lord shall not want any good thing."* (Psalms 34:10). Diligent is showing care and conscientiousness in one's work or duties. To **bear** means to hold up, support, be accountable for, or assume responsibility.

In Proverbs 12:24, God said, if you are diligent, you will rule every aspect of your life. When one is not diligent, he is ruled by flesh and emotions. A lack of diligence equals laziness, but proper planning and preparation will bring prosperity. Jesus died that you may *"bear rule,"* having *"dominion"* over all the things of this world.

Strive to become diligent in your business, and it'll place you in front of great men with resources and opportunities. (Proverbs 22:29) Resist the spirit of *"slothfulness,"* for they shall stand before *"mean men."* Slothful people commonly find themselves **POOR** *(Passing-Over-Opportunities-Repeatedly).*

Remember, God's word overrides the facts; it is "the absolute truth." Therefore, activate your faith in 2016. II Peter 1:3 says, *"God has given you everything pertaining to life and godliness."* So how bad do you want it? Seek God for a "strategy," then pursue it by faith until you recover all. *God wants to blow your mind this year.* But you must first acquire "diligence" concerning the things of God, and ye shall bear rule!

5

PRESERVED FOR A PURPOSE

I Samuel 16:1-13, II Samuel 11:1-1, Psalms 139:14

The church must understand how valuable they are to God. ***Psalms 139:14*** states, *"I praise you because I am fearfully and wonderfully made."* Last week, Minister Austin reinforced how extraordinary the woman's body and reproductive cycle are. Seeing that you're all here listening to these words affirms, *"you're a winner; you made it"*! God called you before the foundation of the world and has *"preserved you for a purpose."* (Jeremiah 1:5). Many of you have gone through great trials and tribulations, but *"the Lord is <u>able</u> to delivereth from him out of them all."* (Psalms 34:19)

Folks have cast you aside and overlooked you, like David, Jessie's youngest son, but God has a plan. Don't give up on your goals and dreams; make a promise to pursue your purpose - push forward. Regardless of past circumstances, look back over your life and thank God for preserving you.

God is sustaining you for something greater – stay focused and agree *"you're a WINNER."* The Lord will sustain those who are obedient to his will for their lives - Stay focused.

6

___

DOING IT GOD'S WAY

ELDER JOYCE TYUS – ASSISTANT PASTOR

I Kings 13:1-24, Exodus 14:13, Romans 6:1-4, Genesis 6:7 & 17:1-19,
Psalms 119:89, Isaiah 55:11, Proverbs 18:21, Revelation 2:29

Saints of God, it's time to do what God told you to do; he's intentional. If you can hear the voice of God, then you have a greater advantage. When God speaks, his words are powerful, direct, and full of life. It's time out for walking in disobedience, gambling your future. The Lord constantly warns his people day after day, week after week, and if you don't listen, there will be consequences. Stop taking him for granted and do what he told you to do. Many of you stand in your own way because of fear and doubt but stand on his spoken word.

God is just and faithful, waiting on you to submit; don't sell him out for stuff. Stop being concerned about what others are doing – Stand still. (Exodus 14:13) Don't go back to those past sins once the Lord has brought you out and imparted a rhema word in your spirit. (Romans 6:1-4)

Form a solid relationship with him today, church. Stop waiting for someone to give you a word but seek the Lord for yourself. Be obedient to the voice and live life more abundantly.

What has God instructed you to do that you haven't done yet? Now is your time to obey God, *repent and live*.

7

____

IT'S TIME TO MOVE OUT OF HERE

THE DROP

I Kings 19:11-13, Psalms 118:24, Proverbs 5 3:5-6, Psalms 139:1-2, Psalms 34:1, Jeremiah 10:23, Psalms 37:23- 37, Psalms 46:10, I Peter 5:6, Job 23:1-14, Genesis 2:18, Job 2:1-10, John 14:26-27

There are so many distractions keeping you from having open communication with God. Sometimes you have to leave everything and *"just drop"* before the Lord. It's time for the family to return to God and bring the altar back home. God sent the Holy Spirit to comfort you and keep you.

The world is in utter chaos; man continues to mess up and refuses to allow the Lord to direct his path. (Proverbs 3:5-6) People are confused, and many believe the creature is wiser than God the Creator. Man must repent and submit to the Lord; *"just drop" and* ask for direction. God is all-knowing. He cannot be figured out. He has to reveal himself. The Lord knows the way you should take. Therefore submit to him and let him lead you to your destiny. (Job 23:10) Keep pushing - Pray Until Something Happens.

8

LORD, I BELIEVE

DON'T DAMN ME

*Matthew 28:18, Mark 18, I Timothy 6:10, John 10:10, Deuteronomy 28:1-68,
Colossians 3:23, Hosea 4:6, Ephesians 4, Revelations 1:17-18 & 20:11-12,
Ecclesiastes 12:1-7*

Unfortunately, you live in the last days, a perilous time where people do not reverence or fear God. Calamity and destruction are all around, and people are doing unthinkable and abominable acts. But thank God Jesus saves! The church must answer the cry of a dying world by exemplifying the father's love and compassion for everyone. An astonishing number of unbelievers are lost and seeking their direction from man instead of God. This community is searching for identity, real love, and kindness, which can all be found in *Christ*. The church must continue to be a safe haven and refuge, a place where God's love and presence abide.

Wake up, Church; don't be damned or ignorant of the enemy's tactics. (Hosea 4:6) There is an enormous need for witnessing, as God has commissioned, to go into the entire world and preach the gospel. (Matthew 28:18-20) The enemy comes to distract you with trivial matters, diverting you from your true purpose, *"kingdom building."*

God is establishing a *"Joshua Generation"* of preachers who'll surrender their will for Christ's sake.

Parents have a tremendous responsibility to mold their children and instill God's word in their hearts. (Psalms 119:11) God is calling you to greatness, but first, you <u>must</u> believe on him and keep his commandments. (John 10:10)

Why should you be dammed when you can be blessed?

9

***

IT'S TIME TO GET OUT OF HERE

I'M TRYING TO FIND GOD, BUT I'M NOT LOOKING HARD ENOUGH

1 Kings 19:11, Job 23:1-10, Isaiah 55:6, Acts 17 Ch., Psalms 37 Ch. & 46:10

This generation has become all too familiar with God. They believe they know him but really don't. Similarly, some Christians believe they can do whatever they want, like sin, without consequences. Then say a couple of *Hail Marys - repent three days for their sins, and they're free.* This is deliberately taking God for granted, and he's not pleased. Many had a great relationship with him initially. Still, they traded him in for something new, like a new car or the latest fashion. You must never stop realizing the value of something you already possess when something new comes along. Job did all the right things yet still experienced great calamity and devastating losses. *Are you doing all the right things? Are you staying in the will of God?* If so, you are not exempt from the bad things this life may bring. These are merely tests and trials you must overcome to develop yourself. Put your confidence in God, trust in Him, and don't stop praying. God has your miracle in a slow cooker, it may take a little longer, but the biggest deal is worth the wait. Stay with God and stop taking him for granted.

10

GOD'S COMMANDMENTS FOR THE CHURCH

Matthew 28:19-20, Romans 10:15-21, I Thessalonians 5:20, John 7:38, Matthew 6:33, Malachi 3:16, Habakkuk 2:3, Psalm 50:12, Hebrew 5:12-14, I John 3:22, Malachi 3:16

Countless Christians have left kingdom living to dabble with the world, doing their own thing. Yet God is still calling for his children to seek him first so that he may "add" and enhance their lives. (Matthew 6:33) As the end times draw near, an influx of evil spirits has been released into the earth, targeting children. The only way to withstand the evil days is with God; you must have *"true deliverance"* and the *"Holy Ghost."* Sin and corruption are all around, but the church must stand for holiness. This is why weekly church services are so important. When entering God's house, you must come with expectation - ready to send up Judah *(praise).*

You must transition from milk to meat at some point in your Christian experience. (Hebrew5:12-14) More often than should, believers are unlearned and inexperienced as it relates to the word of God. Those who should be teachers are still being taught Bible basics, never coming into the knowledge of the truth. (II Timothy 3:7)

How can the church help a sick and dying world when they're sick themselves? God left his spirit, the Holy Ghost, and without it, all are lost. God saved you to do his will on Earth before going to heaven. It's better to be delivered and whole than walk around cute and sick. It's time to get back to the word and follow God's commandments.

11

GOD'S COMMANDMENTS FOR THE CHURCH - PART II

LORD, PULL IT DOWN

II Corinthians 10:3-5, Colossians 3:6, Romans 8:26, II Timothy 3:1-2, Isaiah 55:6, Hebrews 6:18, Malachi 3:16

If you haven't realized you're living in a very social society, there are people and rules wherever you go. Regrettably, this generation struggle with the stronghold of *"entitlement."* This is simply thinking you can have whatever they desire with minimal work or effort. Unfortunately, many parents have done an *injustice* to their children by supplying their every want and desire without establishing a *"foundation of responsibility."* This neglect has developed a group of lazy/helpless folks (stronghold) in urban communities and families.

Walls are designed to hold a structure together. It is also a form of protection; to keep the people within safe and unwanted folks out. We're asking the Lord to *"pull the walls down today."* There have been opportunities and places withheld from our people and community for centuries because of walls of obstruction and discrimination, but they're coming down. The children of Israel saw the mighty wall of

Jericho. They felt inferior, believing they'd never make it over, but God brought the wall down with only their "*SHOUT.*"

When you disobey God's word, you have to deal with God's wrath. Many of you want to go further and pursue excellence yet don't want to go through the uncomfortable process. Remind yourself that this is bigger than you and necessary for your children and generations to come. Lord, pull down the walls!

12

LORD, I NEED A MIRACLE

*Jeremiah 18:1-6, Psalms 46:10, II Corinthians 5:17, Ephesians 6:1,
Deuteronomy 28:1-64, John 3:16, Galatians 6:17, Psalms 118:8,
Jeremiah chapters 1 & 2, Ephesians 5*

Almost everyone in here has been marred or scared by this world. To "mar" is to disfigure or impair the image of. Some of you were scarred by family, abuse, molestation, and rape. These impairments have led to a state of depression and hopelessness, but it's time for the church to put down its distractions and say, "Lord, I Need a Miracle."

Though you're sitting here marred, understand the father can put you back on the potter's wheel and make you whole again. You serve a Mighty God that is more than able to do exceedingly, abundantly above all you can ask or think. What caused you to run from God?

Put it all in his hands and let him fix it. Some of your lives are like bridges, connecting a wretched past to a blessed and holy future in Christ. It is your testimonies that will help others crossover to the other side. So don't shut your mouth during this pivotal time; instead, stand on the mountaintop and testify of God's deliverance and wonder-working power in your life. Submit your ways unto God and allow him to make you better.

13

THE SACRIFICE JESUS MADE

Romans 12:1-2, Revelations 12:1-17, Psalms 107:20, Psalms 100:4,
Psalms 24:1-2, I John 4:19, Matthew 6:24, Genesis 3:8,
Isaiah 14:12-14, John 14:15-31, I Peter 5:6, Matthew 5:16-18

Don't be oblivious, church. You're in a battle, good versus evil. The enemy was cast out of heaven because he felt God was getting too much praise and wanted it for himself. He became lifted up with pride, trying to promote his own agenda. One thing is for certain. God is sovereign. The creature will never be greater than the creator. From the earth were you formed and back to the dirt you'll return. Don't become negatively influenced by the wrong folks getting puffed up with pride; instead, humble yourself under the hand of God that he may establish you. (I Peter 5:6)

Jesus' love was so great that he was the greatest sacrifice. He could have got up from the cross, but he had you on his mind. In this world, you can't mandate people to love you. It must happen willingly. After all, God has done for his people; it's unfortunate that many still don't love him. But will someone make a sacrifice for him today? This world is crazy and terribly wicked and needs a little more light.

Believers let their light shine before men so that they may see your good works and glorify the father. (Matthew 5:16-18) *You'd be nuts not to praise him when you know how he was spit on, beat, mocked, and abused for you and I.* He paid the ultimate sacrifice the least you can do is be thankful and bless his name. (Psalms 100:4)

14

LORD, KEEP ME THANKFUL AND GRATEFUL

*Matthew 5:6, John 4:24, Ezekiel 2 & 3rd, Luke 10:27, Romans 10:17,
Psalms 118:24, Ephesians 4:32*

As the last days persist, you have to be hungry for God's word. Oftentimes, people fail to get in the word until they're in trouble, but that's not his desire. God is looking for consistency from his people. He wants you to seek him while he can be found. (Isaiah 55:6)

Everyone has a spirit but not all walk according to the spirit. You must walk according to the spirit to get a revelation of his word. John 4:24 states, *"they that worship him must worship Him in spirit and in truth."* It is essential to stay rooted in God's word. Having roots means you're grounded and planted in God, immovable. When tests and trials come, they won't overtake or be annulated because you're planted in him. This is the best time to commit to getting rooted in God, be thankful unto him, and bless his name.

15

HIDE ME, JESUS

CO-PASTOR ELLAZEAN JOHNSON

Psalms 57:1-11, Psalms 17:8 & 119:11, Proverbs 18:10, I Samuel 18:5-10,
I Corinthians 15:58, II Thessalonians 2:1-5, Romans 7:18

David was a young man who worked for King Saul and was favored by God. *"David went everywhere that Saul sent him, and did well"*; he was faithful. (I Samuel 18:5) But Saul was jealous of David; he was a man of war and had many talents. An evil spirit from God came upon Saul, and he vowed to kill David. (I Samuel 18:10) Following this event, David, author of Psalms 57, cried out to the Lord, asking for "refuge and protection." God answered and sustained him from the attacks because his heart was fixed on God. With all the issues in the world, believers must stay focused and hide themselves in the father. (Psalms 17:8)

To **_hide_** is to put or keep out of sight; conceal from the view or notice of others. The enemy tries to hide or conceal himself from you. He creeps in subtly (cunningly), but over time his presence increases, causing you to compromise. (Romans 1:28) You're fighting an invisible force. To win, you must fight in the spirit through "spiritual warfare."

The enemy is seeking your soul, but he can't find you if you're in God. (Proverbs 18:10) Establish Christ as the focal point of your life, and he will fight your battles.

16

THE SHEEP ARE OVERFED, AND THE LAMBS ARE STARVING

Zechariah 11:4-17, Acts 86:6-9, Psalms 119:71, Psalms 44:22, I Samuel 15:22, John 21:15, Romans 8:36, II Chronicles 7:14, I Corinthians 14:40, Psalms 127:3, I Peter 4:17, Ezekiel 18:4

Today, most adults (sheep) in the church are overfed and fat on God's word while the children *(lambs)* starve. Ministers, evangelists, and apostles preach to adults worldwide yet overlook the needs of the children who are our future. Unfortunately, many do not understand the importance of depositing in children, forgetting they'll become adults. Kids are often ignored, and many perceive them as difficult, but they have souls too, and all souls belong to the Lord. (Ezekiel 18:4) Thank God for the few folks concerned with instilling a Christian foundation in millennium youth? The enemy is feeding the youth with a ton of useless information, causing them to be slaughtered in droves because of a lack of knowledge. (Hosea 4:6) Teens are being massacred indiscriminately every day in this city, but a change <u>must</u> come.

The church has to take back everything that belongs to them by rethinking what's important.

Judgment is coming to the household of faith; set your house in order before it's too late. (I Peter 4:17)

Many assemblies of faith have shifted their thinking from godliness to worldliness. To walk in the abundance and authority of God, he must be in the center of it all. (I Corinthians 14:40) A prospering church is structured and obedient to the word. (II Chronicles 7:14). Church, it's time to save the lambs.

THIS IS YOUR TIME OF REPENTANCE
JUST DO IT

Matthew 11:28, Matthew 19:26

I just want to remind you; that the Lord is your source and strength. He's there to help and direct you in the direction you should go. However, it requires submission; he'll lead the way and order your steps. Too often, people feel they have life and everything under control, not knowing it's quite the opposite. God educates man through his word, saying, *"Come unto me unto me, all ye that labour and are heavy laden, and I will give you rest."* (Matthew 11:28). God wants to lead you, and without him, you're nothing, but all things are possible through him. (Matthew 19:26) The enemy is striving to get you further and further from your *safety zone*, "the house of the Lord." A backslider doesn't simply walk out the front door. He finds himself moving away from God little by little, slowly becoming immune to secularism and no longer living by the standard of holiness found in God's word. But there's still hope; it's not the end for you. Now's your opportunity to jump back in the word and get close to the "fire" found at the altar of God. Come back to the Lord. Teach his commandments and statues to your children, reciting the *"Shea Prayer"* so they'll never forget all that the Lord has done.

18

FIX IT, JESUS

Psalms 24:16, 51:2-6, 57:7, 101:7, 105:15, Psalms 108:1, 16:9, 118:24, I John 5:3,
I Peter 2:9, John 8:7, 15:5, Romans 8:9, 12:1, Ezekiel 18:4, James 1:15,
I Samuel 16:7, Revelation 3:6, 20:10

You must learn how to lean and depend on God during these difficult times. Saints must stop acting like *"victims,"* scared and helpless, blaming others for their mistakes. Instead, the body of Christ must grow up and mature as God intended. If you change your thinking, then you can change your position. If you have *"trashy"* thinking, there is help for you. Release and dump it at the altar.

King David was a priest, prophet, and king that fell out of grace. He's described as the man after God's own heart, but lust entered his heart once he saw Bathsheba. His actions ultimately led to sin, which brought forth death in his house. (James 1:15) Many are on the front line, and the enemy wants to take you out but remind the devil that you **WIN** in Jesus' name! People of God must become *"believers of action,"* not merely Sunday morning churchgoers. Remember, nothing is going to change until your heart gets fixed. Allow God to come in and fix it today.

Shout to the Lord and say, "Fix Me, Jesus."

19

FIX ME, JESUS

Acts 10:1-10, 25-32, II Peter 3:9, I Thessalonians 5:6, Deuteronomy 3,
Romans 13, Genesis 18:19

As Christians, we expect God to work a miracle when we get to church even though we haven't made him a priority in our home. You can't get all you need in one service. Cornelius was a praying man, and we should all fast and pray for God's will regularly. Don't fool yourself by thinking you can serve the world and God because it's not in your spirit. We can't live contrary to the things of God and expect his favors. We have to be hungry for the Holy Ghost and have a hunger and thirst for God and his righteousness. (Matthew 5:6) The church has become preoccupied with status, gaining recognition, and placing God's plan on the backburner.

But God's will must take persistence over EVERYTHING. Don't forget who brought you out of Egypt. Faith can move God when money and other things can't. It's time to be faithful to him and the Holy Spirit.

20

LORD, SEND DOWN YOUR POWER

Joel 2:28, Acts 2:1, Acts 1:8, Luke 24:49, Matthew 18:20

The first thing Christians must assess is whether they believe God and the power of His word. If you do, ask him to sustain you during these last and evil days. Then, when you go to the father with a request by faith, look for God to come through and deliver SUDDENLY. There's a sound that your church must release to reach the heavens. Deliverance is released when a shout goes forth. It's time for the body of believers to get on one accord in one place with one mind to get the Victory. Stop complaining while you're in the waiting room but worship and rejoice during the wait. Lord, send your power into this place.

21

DANGEROUS DESIRES

JAMES 1:12-15, PSALMS 37:4-5, II TIMOTHY 3:1-7

Today the world is saturated with selfish, self-absorbed, and proud people. Regrettably, this spirit has crept into the modern-day church, which is displeasing to God. Many Christians have exchanged their relationship with God for a religious experience. The saints must evaluate their desires and intentions, keeping them pure. Unfortunately, too many Christians are driven by dangerous desires which flow from the heart. The Lord wants you to give up your will and desires for his. Submit to the Lord, and he will guide your path.

22

———————

WHEN IT'S WELL WITH THEE

Genesis 40:9-14, Deuteronomy 6:1-7 & 8:14-18, Numbers 20:10-12,
Psalms 24:1-2 & 118:24, James 1:3, Romans 8:28

Life is a precious gift, so don't waste time cussing, fussing, and being jealous of others. Joseph experienced this firsthand, being set up by his brothers due to jealousy and hate. He was betrayed, cast into the pit, and later placed in prison because they despised him. They often called him a ***dreamer*** and were jealous because their father favored him. But through his distress, God preserved him during his wilderness experience. After overcoming great obstacles, Joseph was elevated to the 2nd highest position in Egypt. His rough start didn't hinder a successful future; God was with him everywhere. There are many *"dream-killers"* around, but you must look to Jesus through it all. Remember, *"If God birthed something in your spirit,"* he's more than able to bring it to pass (Ephesians 3:20). Disconnect from the haters and align with those pursuing greatness. Understand you don't have to hook and crook to get ahead. When you're walking in the favor of God, you're just *blessed*.

Don't be a Christian with short-term memory, like the butler in Genesis 40th chapter. Don't forget that the Lord brought your family out of Egypt. Stay close to God while in the storm; don't desert him when trouble is over. Never be ashamed of the gospel of Jesus Christ. Let the sounds of Zion bring you out of bondage today. He's waiting to bring you out with his mighty hand!

23

LORD, I NEED TO GET CLOSER TO YOU

Matthew 25:1-13, Luke 14:15-24, Ezekiel 18:4, James 4:5-8, Hosea 4:6, Ephesians 2:1-3, Romans 6:23, Isaiah 59:1-4, Acts 2:38-41, Psalms 90:10-17 & 118:17, Psalms 46:1, II Corinthians 6:14, John 3:16, Exodus 12:23-24, Ecclesiastes 12:1, Revelation 21:23-27

In Matthew 25, there were ten virgins. The Bible indicates that five virgins were wise, and the other five were foolish. Inadequate planning caused the five foolish women to be left behind when the bridegroom returned. They were deceived, believing time was on their side. Procrastination hindered them from walking into their destiny. Countless Christians walk around carrying lamps *"with no oil"* like the foolish virgins, but that is not God's will. Matthew 24:36-44 reveals, *"no man knows the day or hour when the Son of man cometh,"* church get ready. The Lord expects his children to live a holy life, pleasing unto him. Submit your ways to God, and he will help you. (Psalms 37:5-6) Do not allow the thoughts and opinions of man to destroy you, continue to press forward. Every death, catastrophe, and rumor of war should serve as a reminder to get closer to the Lord. Do not ignore his invitation. Reach out to the Lord before it's too late.

24

____

JESUS CAME TO DO A WORK

John 9:1-7, John 6:63, John 4:23, Hebrews 10:25

Jesus came into the world to heal, set free, and deliver but, more importantly, take back everything the enemy stole in the book of Genesis. (John 18:37) Believers find it difficult to praise God because they are still walking in the flesh. Praise leaders have to work extremely hard to get Christians to worship God because many are coming into his presence carnally minded. But the Bible states, *"When the true worshippers shall worship the Father in spirit and in truth."* Jesus came into the world to do a work that his father's will will be done on earth as it is in heaven. All God wants is you. If you are still breathing, you still have time to give God praise. Psalm 150:6 says, *"Let everything that has breath praise the Lord."* The only people exempt from praising him are those who are dead in their graves. Nothing in this world is free. There's an associated cost with everything you do. The church can't survive ignoring God and his statues without correction. "Get in God" and commit your ways unto him, and he will direct your path. Start working for the kingdom!

25

THE POWER OF GOD'S PROMISE

ELDER JOYCE TYUS

Exodus 32:1-14, Ecclesiastes 5:4, Isaiah 55:11, Matthew 4:4, Romans 4:21,
II Corinthians 4:8, Deuteronomy 8

God made a promise with the children of Israel, for they were a *"special people"* unto the Lord. (Deut. 7:6) He took them through the wilderness to prove and humble thee to show what was in their heart. (Deut. 8:2) A *promise* is a declaration or assurance that one will do a particular thing or that a particular thing will happen. When you make God a promise, you become a prisoner to that promise. (Ecc. 5:4)

Believers, you serve a faithful God that cannot lie; he will keep his promise even though you didn't keep your word (Num. 23:19). If God made you a promise and you haven't received it, don't panic. God's promise is a promise; just wait on him. What he has spoken, he shall perform it because he is *God.* (Isaiah 55:11) If your promise has been delayed, it doesn't mean your promise is denied; he's preparing you. Many are anxious to get their promise, but they're not ready for it. As you wait on the manifestation of God's word, say to yourself, *"God prepare me for my promise."* His promise is waiting for you, *"catch up with your promise, because destiny has someplace to be."* The almighty God is more than able to perform that which he has spoken. (Rom. 4:21) Nothing can stop the promises of God. *Get ready for your promise.*

26

GO FORWARD AND FEAR NOT

Genesis 12:1-4, Hebrews 10:25, Malachi 3:16, Matthew 6:33, John 10:27-28, Matthew 7:22-23

Americans are living in extremely tough and crazy times. The world is corrupt and more violent than ever; folks are walking around in a state of *"euphoria* or *escapism."* Too many are committing suicide, battling depression, and losing their minds in the midst of their storms. Sadly, the government hasn't done much to help. Urban communities like Detroit suffer the most, with liquor stores on almost every corner. Medical marijuana dispensaries with neon green signs popping up on every other block in black neighborhoods, adding to the many problems residents face in inner cities. To add insult to injury, minority children are left holding the bag and attending substandard schools with little to no hope of a bright future. Urban residents have been systematically programmed for failure, *but God*.

One thing is for sure. It takes faith and courage to leave family members, homes, and bad habits to seek after the Lord. (Matthew 6:33) In order to go forward, you have to break all unhealthy ties.

Folks will put you in the box if you let them. But what can contain the almighty God if God's spirit is in? Begin to celebrate God, *"you are fearfully and wonderfully."* (Psalms139:14). It takes both faith and courage to push forward. Fear not and keep moving because there is greatness inside of you.

27

GO FORWARD AND FEAR NOT

HE WANTS TO PROSPER YOU

I John 5:14-15, Psalms 1:1-3, Joshua 1:7, Isaiah 55:6-7

According to his word, God promised to bless and prosper you wherever you go and in whatever you do. (Psalms 1:3 & Joshua 1:7) First, for this to happen, you must have faith. Mark 9:23 says, *"All things are possible to him that believeth"*; therefore, wait on God's timing. *"If you ask anything in my name, I will do it,"* says the Lord – so believe on him. (John 14:14)

Why are people so arrogant, preferring to live a substandard life rather than humble themselves to the Lord and live off his benefits and favor? Many are confused and mentally contaminated, hanging with the wrong crowd, stunting their growth because they won't break ties. *"But who shall separate you from the love of God, no one?"* (Romans 8:35-37) Someone is tired of doing it *"their way,"* give it all over to the Lord and let him fix it. Do you want to live in this world without his grace and mercy? Lord forbid, it's time to get it right, for the end is near. Continue to walk with God and let him establish and prosper you.

28

A LABOR OF LOVE

THY WILL BE DONE

*Matthew 6:10, John 4:35, Matthew 9:37-38, John 3:16, II Timothy 3:1-5,
I Timothy 6:10, Mark 8:36-37, II Corinthians 5:14, Romans 8:28 & 12:1,
Psalms 119:11, I Corinthians 13:1-13, Colossians 3:17*

You're sitting here today only because of God's love. His love for you is so great that he sacrificed the life of his *only* son to redeem you back to himself; therefore, he deserves all the praise. John 3:16 says, *"For God so loved the world that he gave his only begotten son."* His love and sacrifice should motivate you to go a little further even when your mind tells you to give up. Perilous times are here according to II Timothy 3:1; men love themselves more than God. Many believers have forsaken Christ and are now dancing with the devil, but God still loves you unconditionally. Be strong and courageous, and let the Lord make you over and fill you with his spirit. (Joshua 1:7)

Stop going through life trying to prove your value and worth to other people. God created, formed, and approved you, and that's all the validation you need. (Romans 8:31) He wants to work through you to fulfill his perfect will, but you *must* make a change. Life is too short to continue in disobedience and regret; get in his will and live off his benefits. Sanctify yourselves, and invest quality time with God so he can direct your path. (Proverbs 3:5-6) Man places his values in many earthly things, but there's nothing in this world greater than God; get to know him before it's too late. The invitation is open to join God's army today.

29

A MISSION OF LOVE

John 3:16-19, Luke 18:1-9, I Corinthians 13:1-13, Hebrews 11:1,
Ephesians 4:29-31, Colossians 3:17, Philippians 2:1-4, Romans 12:19

King David was an anointed man of God and operated in three offices: King, Priest, and Prophet. God's chosen one had become selfish and self-involved. He laid with his captain's wife, impregnated her, and continued to sin to cover up his initial act of infidelity. Driven by ego, David's actions left him in trouble, opening the gateway to sin in his family. Years later, those secret sins brought on dysfunction, causing his children to operate in lies, scandal, and division. His son Amnon had a *strong* desire for his half-sister Tamar, the virgin, and plotted to rape her. (I Samuel 13:1-39) But once his brother Absalom heard of it, he planned to kill Amnon in honor of his sister. Absalom loved Tamar and hated what his brother had done. This forced him to flee his home and become a fugitive.

I pray someone is seeking the Lord for help; start by asking him to close the doors to negative family hurt. This is your opportunity to embrace the word of God and share his love. You must love someone more than yourself and fight for a greater cause; this life is bigger than *YOU*. Your love has to surpass what you want and help those in need; without love, you're nothing. (I Corinthians 13:2) God sent his son to save the world because he loves you, and you must share the same love throughout this world. So start your mission of love.

30

DON'T BE UNSTABLE

ELDER STACY SIMS

James 4:6, I Corinthians 10:21, Colossians 2:6-8, Galatian 6:7-9

You live in a terribly wicked world that's getting worse by the day. Today, God is speaking to his people, saying, *"Be consistent, church, stable."* To be **consistent** means to be steady, reliable, and constant in things of the Lord. On the other hand, inconsistency stems from doubt and fear, but through Christ, you're more than conquerors. (Romans 8:37) The church is the bride of Christ, the living organism of God, commissioned to go into all the world to show forth praise in this wicked and dying world. (I Peter 2:9)

There's a great demand for **Ambassadors** of Christ. This generation is evil. Many are corrupt and confused in the head with no reverence for God. Families are being abused left and right because the devil has a hateful stronghold on them, especially the youth. But you don't have to be weak when God says you are **strong**. (Ephesians 6:10) Accepting Christ as your Lord gives you access to his attributes and characteristics, one being his **dunamis power**. This power gives you the ability to overcome the world's ungodly urges and carnal desires.

Believers of Christ must make a choice; you cannot drink the cup of the Lord and the cup of devils too. (I Corinthians 10:21) Draw nigh to God, and he will draw nigh to you; submit to God, resist the devil, and he will flee. (James 4:6) Let God fix it for you. It's time to get rooted in Christ!

31

PRAYER IS ESSENTIAL IN A CHAOTIC WORLD

ELDER STEVEN BELL

Daniel 6:4, Mathew 11:28, Hebrew 11:1, I Peter 5:7

Daniel demonstrated the importance and authority of prayer. He was a faithful and consistent man that sought the Lord three times a day. I Thessalonians 5:17 advises us to *"Pray without ceasing."* Therefore, it is advantageous for believers to establish a daily *"prayer regimen"* and pray as often as possible.

King Darius made a decree *(mandate)* forbidding anyone to pray or call on their God for thirty days. This may not have concerned some, but it was virtually impossible for Daniel. It was a challenging time for Daniel, if he prayed, he would be thrown into the lion's den, and if he didn't, he would be out of fellowship with God. Nonetheless, Daniel counted up the cost and continued praying and believing God through his trial. Today, many of us are not facing extreme circumstances yet fail to pray to the true and living God. Daniel was more concerned about his ability to pray than getting thrown in the lion's den. In the end, God was with Daniel, and the power of prayer prevailed overall. No matter how chaotic your life may be, a little prayer and consistency will truly see you through.

32

WAKE UP. DO YOU KNOW WHAT TIME IT IS?

ASSISTANT PASTOR JOYCE TYUS

Judges 16:5-20, Romans 13:11-14, Isaiah 52:1-2 & 40:8, Matthew 26:39-47,
Lamentations 3:22-23, I Peter 1:21, Luke 20:33, Acts 2:38, Nehemiah 8:10,
Ephesians 6:11

Sampson the Nazarite was a strong and mighty warrior that allowed his heart to cloud his vision. Aware of Delilah's ill intentions, he turned a blind eye to deceit to fulfill his own lust, weakening him. These actions caused Sampson to be spiritually blind long before the Philistines blinded him naturally. His overall negligence caused him to lose his power and anointing. Ask yourself, *"What's binding me, keeping me asleep and emotionally unaware of what's going on?*

The climate of the world is steadily diminishing, and shootings and terrorism are at an all-time high. People are helpless and afraid, searching for answers, yet the church is *asleep.* Many would ask, *"How can the church sleep at a time like this?"* The world, including the church, has allowed the devil to create a false sense of time, bamboozling and distracting them by life's circumstances. People feel they have 20-30 years to get their salvation together, but *"YOU DO*

NOT" time is drawing near. The world is taking God's mercy for granted, and he's soon to return. God wants to impart his word in you today; nothing is as powerful and prevailing as the word of God. He brought you out of so much. So don't go back and risk it all to dance with the devil. Wake up, church, prepare yourself, get in position, get up from your state of slumber. *Do you know what time it is?*

33

TOO MUCH TOO SOON

LUKE 15:11-32, JOB 39:5-8, GENESIS 25:29-33,

Romans 7:18, Joshua 24:15, John 3:16

No man knows the day or hour when the Lord will return; therefore, you must use time wisely and responsibly. There was a certain man who had two sons. The younger son asked his father for his inheritance. It is not customary to distribute the inheritance before the father's death, but the father complied with his son. The son left his hometown with all his goods and wealth and spent his inheritance within days on riotous living. The son became a citizen in a foreign land and worked to survive. While out feeding the hogs, the son became hungry, having a strong desire to eat what the pigs were eating in the hog pen. He began to reflect on how his father's hired servants lived in better conditions. He desired to go home and repent to his father for his actions; *he came to himself.* Is someone sitting here living beneath what God desires for you?

Though you may bring reproach to God's name by misrepresenting him around your family or friends, he still loves you and won't abandon you. Many can testify of his sustaining power when looking back over our lives. Time is short; you need to run for your life. Your destiny depends on it. Ask God, *"What is his will for your life?"* Someone needs to refresh today and come back to Christ.

34

WHAT ROAD AM I ON?

YOU WON'T HAVE TO WALK ALONE

Luke 24:15, Proverbs 12:15, Proverbs 10:19

You must watch the spirits you entertain because they can take root if you don't rebuke them. On average, people are more prone to focus on the negative things in life versus the positive. Don't allow your mind to be stuck on your storm, hurt, or betrayal while ignoring that God is with you all the time. What's hindering, causing you to miss out on the things God has promised you? It's time to focus on the good rather than the bad and become an *optimist* in the kingdom. How long will it take you to figure out that God is with you in every step you take?

Starting today, **stop** focusing on one who's *not* with you but concentrate on who has your back. You're not alone, *"This is the day the Lord has made,"* so enjoy it and live your best life. (Psalms 118:24)

September 2, this year

35

STAY ON THE RIGHT ROAD

GPS – GOD'S PURPOSE STATION

Proverbs 16:25, Proverbs 3:5-6, Matthew 7:13-14, Acts 9:1-20, Exodus 14:13,
I Timothy 6:10, James 4:14, I Peter 2:9, Romans 3:23, Jeremiah 31:3

God has given you a GPS – *"God's Purpose Station,"* designed to keep you on track. A GPS is designed to assist you on the road of purpose and destiny in God. A **road** is a path, a wide way leading from one place to another, a series of events or a course of action that will lead to a particular outcome. God has given you dominion and authority on the earth; therefore, you don't have anything to fear. The enemy is an accuser of the brethren; his job is to overwhelm you with situations and circumstances. So many people fail to see the beauty of today because they're focused on the past. The church has become numb and fickle in its beliefs, but it's time to get back on track. God will keep your mind in perfect peace if you keep it stayed on him. Being connected to Jesus is the greatest name above all names. The devil wants to devour you, but God is your refuge and strength. Salvation is your vehicle through this life, so grab hold. So many will get off their road for a man/woman, a shiny car, or other material things. But you don't have to go the wrong way. When God tells you to do something, do it! Stay focused and continue on the right road.

36

WHOSE REPORT WILL YOU BELIEVE?

Numbers 13:30-33, I John 5:13-15, Philippians 2:5,
Hebrews 11:6, Psalms 50:12, Proverbs 10:22

When pursuing your godly purpose, you can't run around asking for everyone's opinion or validation. Anytime you're on the path of destiny, snares and tribulations will come but keep pushing. Stop speaking defeat to yourself based on what Satan or man said. *What did God say? If he said it, that settles it.* Don't accept less than what God has for you. Folks will rob you of your faith if you let them, watch the company you keep. Change comes through prayer, there's power in prayer, and it's essential in your Christian walk.

The question of the day is, *"Whose Report Will You Believe?"* The devil is vigilant and relentless in his pursuits to take you down, but you must place *"faith over facts."* Faith overlooks opposition and issues. While faith operates on the word of God, *"For faith comes by hearing and hearing by the word of God."* (Romans 10:17). The enemy wants to discourage you and stop your praise and worship. It doesn't matter what the devil said or what seed he's planted in your mind; get a word from the Lord. The Bible declares, *"We are more than conquerors through him who loves us"; "You're a Champion!"* (Romans 8:35-39) God's report declares you're healed, free, delivered; you have the Victory. *"If God said it, when will you claim it?"* Again, *whose report are you going to believe?*

37

FASTEN YOUR SEATBELT. THE ROAD IS ABOUT TO GET BUMPY.

Romans 13:11-13, Galatians 5:13, Hebrew 6:10, Matthew 7:21-23, John 1:10

Today's church must prepare for the bumps and turbulence of life. Sadly, many Christians have taken off their seatbelts for various reasons leaving them open and unprotected for the collisions of life. Whenever you pledge to walk with the Lord, expect to be kicked along the way but hang in there. Believers are getting attacked on every hand, and storms are all around, but God is telling his people, *"Don't abandon ship."* Though you're in turbulence, realize you'll make it through, even if it's *on broken pieces.* Fortify yourself with God's armor and trust him through the process. Understand that your faith will be tested, but you will be victorious if you keep your seatbelt on. God's seatbelt is his word - it'll uphold you in unstable times. Someone needs to hold on to God's word today, which is everlasting and settled in heaven. Have you invested quality time with God in prayer? Has he given you a confirmation that he's with you no matter what? II Thessalonians 2:2 says, *"Be not shaken in mind or troubled by words or letters"* cause the adversary comes *"to kill, steal, and destroy, but God comes to give you an abundant life."* (John 10:10)

Believers, learn how to control your emotions by turning problems into praise. When God has a purpose for you, nothing can stop it. So stay with God, church; buckle your seatbelts because things will get bumpy.

38

THE SOUL THAT WAS MORE IMPORTANT THAN THE PIG.

Mark 5:8-9, II Peter 3:1-8, Matthew 6:33, Psalms 23:1, I Timothy 6:6-10, II Corinthians 5:17, Psalms 118:24

Today people are more concerned about pigs than souls. In this case, the *"pig"* is an analogy for any material thing that exists in the world (i.e., house, money, husband/wife, etc.). The *"pig"* is generally something you treasure above anything, your number one priority in life. The church has lost focus, seeking everything but the God that saved them from annihilation. The Lord is saying today, *"Where are my people? For I have picked them up, but they have let me down; where are my people?"* Stop giving God what doesn't cost you. It's not a sacrifice he wants you.

The Bible says, *"All souls are Gods,"* for ministries to remain vibrant and alive, they must *reproduce*. (Ezekiel 8:4) The church should continuously stay pregnant, bringing forth children; *focused on souls over pigs.* How can you have a successful future if you're stuck in the past? Stop talking about those old dead things and move forward. God wants to do great things. Praise your way to deliverance. Don't place things over people. Instead, value relationships and cherish the only life you have to live. Your life is more important than the pig!

39

THE POWER OF LOVE

LOVING THE CREATOR MORE THAN THE CREATURE

Malachi 3:14, Genesis 12:1-3, Galatians 5:7, Hebrew 11:25,
I Corinthians 15:16, John 6:53, I John 4:7-8, John 15:15-17, I Peter 4:8,
Isaiah 43:1-2, Proverbs 21:2, Galatian 3:1, Colossians 3:23-24

The word of God reveals the power of love, for *"God is love."* (I John 4:8) He shares his love with his people so that everyone will have access to him. This world is filled with so many distractions, especially with the internet and social media, but you must remain focused like Jesus. Focus on your assignment; don't let others deter you from the road God's placed you on. Repent; don't allow sin for a season to destroy your entire future. *"The greater the test, the greater the blessing."*

As children of faith, you must be wise and rooted in God's word. You are his chosen, don't let the world bewitch you, separating you from God's love. If the ways of this world get in your head, it'll get in your heart and ultimately get in your spirit. No one will be there or have your back like God will. (I John 4:19) *Must God contend for your love? "I have picked you up, but you let me down,"* saith the Lord. Stop being judgmental towards one another and walk in God's perfect love; forgive those who have wronged you. Don't let your faults keep you out of his favor.

40

LOOKING BEYOND NOW

Genesis 25:29-32, Psalms 34:3, Deuteronomy 28:1-16, Philippians 4:19, Proverbs 29:18, I Corinthians 2:9, Psalms 30:5, Isaiah 59:19, Hebrew 11:25, Acts 28:3, Psalms 101:3, Romans 12:3, Joshua 24:13

In Genesis chapter 25, Esau made the worst decision of his life without thinking. He sold his birthright for a pot of soup, never looking at the big picture, but he was focused on *"now."* Unfortunately, this resulted in him missing out on the abundance of blessings. Instead, his brother Jacob received this father's blessings and inheritance on his sickbed.

People today thought what they left God for was worth it, but they've lost more than they gained. It's essential never to put anyone or anything above God, for he is the source and the father of all things. Stop making decisions in the heat of the moment but consider the consequences; count up the costs. (Hebrew 11:25) Daily, many of you encounter folks driven by their emotions; some are ticking time bombs. All it takes is one wrong decision to cause a life to be lost or a family to be torn apart; a choice could change your entire future. Life is too short to play games; think before acting or reacting. Don't give up on God. He has more for you; greater is coming. Forgive today; shake those negative thoughts off and pursue a future of purpose.

41

WHAT DO YOU NEED TO PULL DOWN & WHAT ARE YOU DOING ABOUT IT?

LORD, TEACH ME HOW TO FIGHT

Psalms 68:1 & 144:1, Ephesians 6:10-20, Matthew 6:33 &16:26, Romans 13:11, II Corinthians 10:3-4, Isaiah 58:1-8

If you didn't know before, you're in a spiritual battle, and the church must wake up. Many are losing battles because they don't understand warfare. It's time to stop fighting in the flesh and learn to war in the spirit. The Bible states, *"For we wrestle not against flesh and blood."* (Ephesians 6: 10). No more battling with family, coworkers, and foes. Instead, focus on *Satan,* the real enemy.

Another reason saints are losing wars is lack of preparation. Saints are out of shape, obese outside, while starving spiritually inside. It's time to make sacrifices before God by fasting and praying. Push your plate aside and spend more quality time with the Lord. Take back what belongs to you, walking through your home rebuking devils and unclean spirits. Arise out of the slump and put on your armor of protection. Get back in position and fight for your children in future generations. Psalm 68:1

Utilize the dunamis power he's equipped you with. Lord, teach your people to fight and pull down strongholds in Jesus' name!

42

JESUS CAME TO DO A WORK

John 9:1-7, John 6:63, John 4:23, Hebrews 10:25

Jesus came into the world to heal, set free, and deliver but, more importantly, take back everything the enemy stole in the book of Genesis. (John 18:37) Believers find it challenging to praise God because they are still walking in the flesh. Praise leaders have to work extremely hard to get Christians to worship God because many are coming into his presence carnally minded. But the Bible states, *"When the true worshippers shall worship the Father in spirit and in truth."* Jesus came into the world to do a work that his father's will will be done on earth as it is in heaven. All God wants is you. If you are still breathing, you still have time to give God praise. Psalm 150:6 says, *"Let everything that has breath praise the Lord."* The only people exempt from praising him are those who are dead in their graves. Nothing in this world is free. There's an associated cost with everything you do. The church can't continue to survive ignoring God and his statues without correction. "Get in God" and commit your ways unto him, and he will direct your path. Start working for the kingdom!

43

WAR AND WORSHIP

Joshua 6:9-18, 7:1, Psalms 46:10, 47:1, II Chronicles 20:17, I Peter 5:8

War is combat between two opponents. Most wars start because someone wants what the other one has. We all face challenges and will experience various battles in our lifetime, but God! The enemy is a bully seeking out the weakest link, someone not equipped to fight. No fight should be taken for granted. The enemy is a roaring lion seeking whom he may devour. (I Peter 5:8) Never underestimate your enemy. Christians, it's time to war and worship in your battle. To be a real warrior, you must present your body as a living sacrifice by watching, praying, and praising.

Joshua knew he was outnumbered and surrounded in a strange land, but he was preserved for a purpose. You can't win this battle by cussing and arguing with folks or posting negative comments on Facebook. If you want to get God's attention, start worshipping. This is not a carnal battle but a spiritual one. You're so smart or strong to where you can fight alone. There's nothing too hard for God to handle. So keep praising through the turbulent times. Your praise will cause you to win the war.

44

THIS IS NOT THE SEASON OR TIME TO GIVE UP ON GOD

Philippians 4:8, Romans8:10, Ecclesiastes 3:1-8

Ecclesiastes 3:1-8 tells us that there is a time and season for everything under heaven. Many of you have lost your faith in God. But frankly, this is not the time. Now is not the time to lose hope or to stop praying. Church, please don't stop praying or worshipping the God of peace during a turbulent time in society. Whatever has troubled your mind, the heavenly father can handle it. The enemy wants you to lose, so you won't gain what God has promised.

Romans 8:10 says, *"The joy of the Lord is your strength."* The Holy Ghost will give you strength and peace to face what lies ahead. It's time out from coming in the house, hearing the word, and returning home the same way. Don't let the enemy hold you down; receive total deliverance. Don't give up on God because he won't give up on you.

45

────

YOU BETTER KEEP GOD IN FRONT OF YOU

Joshua 3:1-4, Psalms 46:10, 122:1, 116:12, Colossians 3, Hebrew 10:25, Matthew 26

We live in a time where too many Christians are staying home getting their word from television and YouTube. He didn't save us just to stay home but called us out of darkness to assemble ourselves. It's time to stop putting God in the rear. Every time you have an opportunity testify of his goodness and grace. The word says, *"What shall I render unto the Lord for all His benefits toward us?"* (Psalms 116:12). We can't put God to the side when everything is going well and only call when in trouble. When you place God in the rear, the perception is that you want to be in front. Remember, only what you do for Christ will last. God won't take the wheel and be in the rear at the same time. It's time to move ahead and get on one accord. Just step back and let God take control.

46

"DROP" – DELIVERANCE, RESTORATION, OVERCOMING THROUGH PRAYER

Matthew 26:36-40, Romans 10, Isaiah 53:5,
Isaiah 5:14, Romans 8:26-28, Psalms 30:5

Do you know you are blessed to have the ability to take everything to the Lord in prayer? To DROP is to cast all your cares upon him and spend intimate time with the father. (I Peter 5:7) When you pray to him in secret, he'll bless you openly. (Matthew 6:4) If you don't know what to pray for, the Bible says the spirit will make intercession for you. (Romans 8:26) The church must establish a prayer life separate from corporate prayer. Corporate prayer is in a controlled environment where you're instructed to participate; it's protocol. But during this season, you must go into your secret closet and bless the Lord, now's the time to spend secret time with God. When you seek the Lord, you'll find him. He wants to talk to you early in the morning. Don't neglect to call him; your soul wants to communicate with God. God wants to "restore"; stop thinking you have it all together. Take God out of the rear and put him in front.

Down there, you'll get restoration and "rest." You can't get rest from stressing and worrying. The Bible says, "*all those who are heavy laden,*

I'll give you rest." Don't find your rest in nicotine, the hookah lounge, or weed. Find comfort in Jesus. Church, don't stop praying; pray and then pray some more. Wait on your miracle, deliverance, and breakthrough. It's on the way!

47

PRAISE & WORSHIP PRODUCES BLESSINGS & FRUIT

Psalms 34:1, Romans 12:11-12, Romans 22, Psalms 47:1, Psalms 50

Psalms 34:1 says, "*I will bless the Lord at all times, and his praise shall continually be in my mouth.*" There is a praise in the house, but are you too lazy and burdened to praise God? The church has become too comfortable with their salvation. They often forget and sit down on the God who brought them out. It's time to say, "*Lord, it's me.*" You don't have the right to abort what God has birthed in you. If the church does not praise God, then who will? There will be a time when you feel forsaken but keep praising him. You can praise yourself out of a dry field. No good thing lasts forever, and no bad thing will last forever. If you want to come out of the Hell you are in, PRAISE HIM. Praise him like you have lost your mind. Praise him for who he is and not just for what he gives. Praise Him for his many blessings, boast about his unconditional love, grace, and mercy; magnify his Holy Name. Let's Praise and worship him not just today but every day.

48

———

HE'S ALREADY FORGOTTEN WHAT YOU CAN'T FORGET

Psalms 103:10-11 & 137:1-6, Titus 3:1-7, Micah 7:19, Isaiah 1:18, Ezekiel 18:19-21, I Peter 2:9, Revelation 12:10-11

Everyone in this life sound of my voice has a past. Still, you must discover your purpose to pursue a greater tomorrow. So many wander aimlessly, trying to find themselves, not understanding their purpose in God. You were created to be a praise unto him in heaven and the earth. God wants to wash you of your sins today, *"for the wages of sin is death; but the gift of God is eternal life through Jesus Christ our Lord."* (Romans 6:23). Let him free your mind; stop holding yourself back by living in the past and press for a brighter tomorrow. Make a wise decision to live for Christ today.

49

WATCH OUT FOR THE DEVIL'S TOOLBOX

Revelation 12:9-12, I Timothy 6:10, Romans 8:28, Ecclesiastes 10:19, Matthew 6:33, Isaiah 14:13, Matthew 6:33, Matthew 7:2, Ezekiel 33:31-33

Life is too short to sit around being idle. The devil has a number of tools and tricks in his toolbox. These devices are used regularly to distract God's children, preventing them from achieving their godly destiny. Two prevalent tools are envy and jealousy. The enemy uses them to divide people worldwide, especially in the church. Envy has grown immensely due to social media and the expansion of the internet; now, it seems like everyone is in competition with one another. Envy sets in when folks are unhappy and unfulfilled, causing them to desire the lives, relationships, and material possessions of others. This is a significant issue in the modern church and threatens the true love and fellowship of the saints. Another tool is strife which is simply anger, bitterness, and conflict. These strategies keep thousands of people from living peaceful and fulfilled lives. Strife prevents men from having pure friendships due to conflict and strife. The devil came to divide the world, but Jesus came to save it and bring souls back to him. The church cannot afford to follow in the footsteps of the world being envious but must lead the world to Christ. Start spreading the good news of Christ by loving and appreciating one another.

50

THE D'S IN THE DEVIL'S TOOLBOX

Matthew 12:25, John 17:20, Colossians 3:22-24, Psalms 118:24, 101:7, & 14:1,
Hosea 4:6, Romans 12:1, Proverbs 16:18, II Chronicles 16:9,
Psalms 84:10 & 53, Hebrew 11:6, I John 2:16, James 1:5,
Romans 13:1 & 8:35-39, Philippians 2:5 & 4:12, Revelation 2:16

The enemy is a crafty serpent that desires to destroy God's people with his deadly toolbox. Some of his greatest tools begin with a *D: division, depression, and deceit* are just a few.

Division is to be separate; the absence of unity which is *not* of God. If God is in the midst, then the devil wants to divide.

The next *D* is *Depression, an intense, prolonged feeling of* sadness and worthlessness brought on by the environment or life events. It can leave one with a negative mental state, even suicidal. One fact is that you can't stay depressed when the Holy Spirit and God's praises are in you.

Deceit is another device, the practice of deceiving others through dishonesty and misleading tricks, oftentimes for material gain.

Many will put possessions over relationships to achieve the enemy's plan. *Secular humanism* is on the rise, but the church has to push God's mission of *Christianity* over its own plan. Church, don't be a *fool*, those who run off emotions and are irrational but be vigilant and sober-minded in God. (Psalms 14:1) Choose to stand on the Lord's side. His word has sent warnings; take heed before it's too late.

51

THE D'S IN THE DEVIL'S TOOLBOX - PART II

*Matthew 12:25, Psalms 118:24, 101:7, Hosea 4:6, John 17:20,
I Corinthians 14:33, Ephesians 5:25-28*

As saints of the most high God, it's important not to fall for the devil's tricks. The enemy constantly uses the device called *"division"* to divide and separate the household. He can use your children, husband, or even you to fulfill his plan. I Corinthians 14:33 says, *"For God is not the author of confusion, but of peace, as in all churches of the saints."* It's easy for the devil to use division when the saints lack a steady prayer life. Have you prayed and praised God today? Problems and trouble can knock the shout out of you, but the **HOLY GHOST** gives you *power*; activate it. (Romans 15:13) Stop crying and start **PRAISING**; life is too short. Stop wasting time being miserable, worrying, and gossiping. Husbands and wives, it's time to touch and agree, exemplify agape love, and appreciate one another. Don't prostitute your relationship or let the devil use you. Stay in the will of God; you're always on his mind.

52

WITH GOD, I CAN

NUMBERS 13:26-30, PHILIPPIANS 4:13, MATTHEW 17:20,

Hebrews 10:25, Psalms 27:14

Regardless of the weapons and forces that may be against you, recognize that God is <u>more than able</u> to *strengthen* you for the victory. (Philippians 4:13) When equipped with the *Holy Ghost*, nothing is impossible with Christ working inside you. (Luke 1:37) As you think about your present tests and trials, remember, *"God is bigger than that."* During your storm, embrace the pain/discomfort by singing praises and encouraging yourself in the Lord; He is a *present help*. (Psalms 46:1)

God is calling you to be a *consistent* witness for him; *"go into the highways and compel men to come in."* (Luke 14:23). Do not become bombarded with the cares of this world as the ungodly; instead, *"cast your cares upon him for he careth for you."* (I Peter 5:7) God promised Abraham he would bless his seed, and it came to pass. The devil knows you're BLESSED, which is why he's relentless in his attacks towards you but *"don't lose focus."* You're waiting on promises, but giants are sitting on them; remember, *Giants do Fall*. Don't be discouraged by the test of time. Hold on. God made you GREAT; *speak his words* over your life. "*Wait on the Lord: be of good courage, and he shall strengthen thine heart: wait I say, on the Lord.* (Psalms 27:14) With God, you can!

PART II

1

———

AWAKE ZION/CHURCH
THE SLEEPING CHURCH

Isaiah 51:1-9 & 52:1:19, Ezekiel 3:2 & 33:1-6, Joel 2:1-15, Romans 13:11-16, Revelation 2:17 & 19:7, I Timothy 4:17, Ephesians 2:2, Romans 13:11, Proverbs 6:9, Ephesians 5:23, Matthew 24:43

Today's society is busier than ever; people are not getting enough sleep leading to short attention spans. Some feel they've been wronged and are walking around bitter and upset. In I Peter 5:7, God says, *"Cast all your cares upon me"*; remember, this is a spiritual fight, and God can handle it. The world is perverse. The prince of the air has poured out the spirit of lust through TV, the internet, and music. Social media have distracted so many creating a false sense of reality. Folks are too trusting looking to fit in when they've been chosen.

God saw the condition of his people and sent the servant Ezekiel to warn them. God's desire is for none to perish; he left the church with a pastor to be the watchman on the wall to warn his people of what's to come. Zion, now it's high time. It's not time to slumber, but wake up and get it together. (Romans 13:11)

2

____

LORD, THANK YOU FOR ALLOWING ME TO TOUCH YOU

Mark 5:25-34, John 4:7-25, Ephesians 2:2-7

To _touch_ is to come so close to or come into contact with another or thing. Generally, people will only touch folks they're comfortable with or have permission to embrace. It would be abnormal to go around touching people you didn't know. It would be an illegal offense punishable by law. However, the Bible's illustration of _touch_ is often referred to as _healing from the Lord._ In Mark 5:27, the woman with the issue of blood was bonded with this ailment for 12 long years, but her condition instantly changed with one touch from the Master. Some of you may be trapped and entangled with the yoke of bondage, but God is more than able to deliver you out of it all. (Psalms 34:19) Once upon a time, you were a sinner and didn't know God, but a touch from him turned your life completely around. Someone in this place must let go of the past to receive a touch from God. People will often try to hold you hostage to previous faults and hang-ups, but God is a DELIVERER calling you to greatness.

The deliverer is here; get yours so those connected with you can get free too!

3

SLEEPING ON THE JOB

*Matthew 26:36-38, Galatians 6:7-9, Hebrews 12:14, Joel 2:1 & 2:15-16,
Psalms 127:1 & 37:25, Romans 10:13, Proverbs 10:12*

Folks are increasingly self-centered, focused primarily on their needs and concerns. Jesus was accommodating and concerned with each person even when no one had his back. Psalms 127:1 except the Lord build a house, they labor in vain, is God in your house? Put out deception, hate, and bitterness to make room for God's fruit of the spirit joy, love, peace, and righteousness. The church is asleep, unconscious of what's happening in the house, and the saints are sleepwalking. Too many are coming to church out of routine and fellowship with no intentions of changing. Fall in love with the creator and establish a relationship with him. The world wants to steal the *voice* of the church and block your praise from reaching heaven. The unsaved will act foolishly during games and concerts and then mock and criticize the church for making a joyful noise unto the Lord. Wake up, Zion; the signs are all around. Blow the trumpet, know who you are, and watch for the enemy's devices. If you don't retreat, you'll get a treat. God has brought you this far by faith and will award your faithfulness, wake up, church. There's work to do.

4

UNTITLED

Matthew 13:45-52, John 8:32, I Peter 2:9, Psalms 14:1-3, Psalms 24:5-10, Hebrews 10:38, Hebrews 12:6, Romans 10:17, Psalms 37:1 & 37:37, I Corinthians 15:58, Ecclesiastes 9:11, John 17:1-36, Psalms 119:11

Everyone in this life is on a journey, daily creating history, but ultimately death is the final destination. During this life, it is important to impact those around you positively. You have only one life to live. Therefore, live on purpose. It's not easy living a life of holiness in a carnal and humanistic society. Many people turn to Facebook, Instagram, TV, and other forms of entertainment to escape the day-to-day issues life may bring. But God is calling his children back to him. I Peter 2:9 declares, *"You are a royal priesthood, an holy nation, a peculiar people"*; God chose you for his glory. It doesn't take much effort to act like the ungodly (worldly), yet it takes work to be holy, sanctified, and *set apart*. Therefore, the church must get back to the basics, the word of God **(BIBLE)** – Basic Instruction Before Leaving Earth. (Romans 10:17) God has a purpose for your life and wants to change your destiny. Surrender everything to the Lord today so he can help you along this journey.

5

UNWRAP THE GIFT

IT'S TIME TO ELEVATE

MARQUIS CARTER JR.

II Corinthians 6:17, I Peter 5:6

To be elevated, you must be separated. God wants to speak, but you won't spend quality time alone with him. To go higher in God, you must have **SPE - *Separation, Preparation, and Elevation.*** So don't get scared and rush the process, experience, and growth on the journey. Get spiritual; you'll reap in due time. It's time to move to the next level; this is the year of the youth.

6

BE FREE

CHARLES BRYANT

Philippians 4:13, Roman 11:29, Hebrew 11:1, Matthew 11:12

A *gift* is something that is given to you. How can you unwrap the gifts God placed inside when you're handcuffed or in prison? Until you're free, you can't unwrap your gifts. Be *free,* loosed, liberal, unbound; someone came in bound, but liberation is in the house. Speak the word with authority, free your mind using the power to lose those bound areas. Take your stuff back and leap for joy; be free today.

7

THE GIFT LOOKS GOOD ON YOU

AMAYIA BATES

II Timothy 1:1-7, Acts 1:8

Apostle Paul is speaking to Timothy, reminding him of the gifts inside of him and how the world needs to know of them. Timothy's mother and grandmother laid hands on him to stir up the fire on the inside, what your parents are trying to do. The gift inside will unleash the power and spiritual flames you've had since birth. The Holy Ghost is a gift only God can give. Millennials don't walk in performance as secular artists but walk in the power of God. Make sure you have the Holy Ghost so your gift can be wrapped with his *power*.

IROCK YOUTH

8

YOU DON'T HAVE TO FALL

Jude 1:1-24, John 8:32, I Corinthians 15:58, I Peter 4:18, Isaiah 54:17, Psalms 24:9, Romans 10:17, Job 14:14, Matthew 6:11, Psalms 37:5, Revelation 12:10, Isaiah 40:31, Genesis 50:20, Proverbs 16:8, Matthew 6:33, Ephesians 3:20

As a believer of Christ, you must be consistent and steadfast in your daily walk. Life brings on many seasons, which you must prepare to handle. The church is in jeopardy and must continue to *"go out into the highways and hedges,"* making disciples. (Luke 14:23) Continue to *"fight the good fight of faith"* and *contend for your faith.* (I Timothy 6:12) The Lord sent his word. Therefore, you don't have to fall. Simply surrender and commit to making a change to the person God ordained you to be. It's imperative that you re-present Christ in the world *and "be steadfast and unmovable."* (I Corinthians 15:58)

Why would you swap the *Savior* of the world for *Satan,* a murderer? Satan tried to exalt himself over God, but it didn't work. Don't allow the lack of power to cause you to lose your position in God. Stop catching *hell* and rebuke it with the word of God; speak the word.

God gave you the power to withstand the gates of hell. Use your authority. Do not become envious and jealous of anyone; _You Are Great_. The Bible states, _"You're fearfully and wonderfully made"_; created in his image. (Psalms 139:14)

Whose report will you believe?

$$9$$

HOLY COMMUNION

Psalms 118:24, Matthew 26:17-30, I Corinthians 11:24

Communion: This is *a holy time of worship* when we corporately come together as one body to remember and celebrate what Christ did for us. We observe Communion because **the Lord told us to.** We are to obey his commandments outlined in his word, *"And when he had given thanks, he brake it, and said, Take, eat: this is my body, which is broken for you: this do in remembrance of me."* (I Corinthians 11:24)

In observing Communion, we remember *Christ* and all he has done for us in his life, death, and resurrection. When observing Communion, we take time to *examine ourselves, "But let a man examine himself, and so let him eat of that bread, and drink of that cup."* (I Corinthians 11:28)

We are also proclaiming his death until he comes. It is, then, a statement of faith. When we observe Communion, we show our participation in the body of Christ. Jesus died that we may live. Therefore we, the church of God, shall live a life that reflects Christ.

Remember his death daily and worship him, for he has done great things!

10

GOD IS GETTING READY TO CHANGE THE SEASON
SEASON CHANGE

*Isaiah 10:27, Isaiah 55:6-9, II Corinthians 7:10, II Corinthians 4:3,
Romans 6:1, I Samuel 15:23, I Corinthians 5:5, Hebrews 12:14,
II Chronicles 7:14, I Peter 4:17, II Thessalonians 2:3,
Isaiah 4:1, Romans 7-10 chapters*

God is warning the church to get in position and sanctify your house. He spoke through the man of God, saying, "Come out of the crowd, turn from those carnal-minded folks, and hold fast to his word." When you fail to listen to his voice, trouble will come to get your attention, like in Exodus with the children of Israel. You can't serve God without ***meeting his conditions.***

Often, parents can over accommodate their children aiding them knowing they're stubborn and disobedient. But God rebuked Samuel for mourning Saul's defiance. You can't change the mindset of someone walking in disobedience. ***Only God and trouble can*** so stop losing sleep. God said he's taking the yoke off today, but it happens through an ***obedient spirit.*** The battle is on, ***don't*** stop praying cause quitting's not on the agenda. Put it all in God's hand and watch him work.

11

IT'S TIME FOR CUSHI TO RUN

II Samuel 18:19-33, Ephesians 4:22-32, Genesis 9:9-29, I Corinthian 3:16-18

Cushi was a black man selected to deliver a sensitive message to King David. Absalom, David's son, became a fugitive after killing his brother. Shortly after, the king allowed him to return home, where he coveted his father's position. Absalom and his entourage rose up against David but were defeated by the king's army in the woods. Someone had to deliver the sad news to the king, and Cushi was selected. Others around wanted to take the message, but it was Cushi's time to run and deliver the word.

This is Cushi's season. There's a Cushi in the building with a word for the people. As Black History Month ends, we honor the biblical patriots that came before us. So don't become stagnant, folks. Get busy pursuing your godly purpose. Run Cushi run. It's your season.

12

SECRET PRAYER/ PRIVATE PRAYER

Jeremiah 33:3, Psalm 91:1, Matthew 6:5, Isaiah 26:3

There is a private place where God wants to meet you. It's in prayer. There are secrets that we don't want to be revealed. But God knows us privately. So it's time to get off Facebook and Instagram. Stop watching so much television and get into God. God wants to talk to you privately and manifest great things in you, but these habits and distractions have all your time. These things were designed to keep you carnal.

There is a secret place where you should dwell. This does not come from public prayer but from private prayer. So, it's time to spend some private time with him. No one can reveal anything about you but God. We all need to get delivered at home before we come to church. Are you connecting with God? Step into the spirit. Go a little further. God is getting ready to change your season. He is giving you a preview.

13

THE CHRISTIAN SHOPPING LIST, THE PASTOR'S SHOPPING LIST

Amos 3:3, Psalm 42:1, Matthew 4:4, 6:11, 1 Peter 2:1,
Romans 15, II Timothy 2: 3-7

In 1 Corinthians 3, Paul was sent to the city of Corinth, where the people were canal and followed idolatry. Paul heard of their carnality and division and was there to teach them holiness.

Today we live in a world where the eyes and ears are never full. If God is going to use you, you have to have control. Just because you have the means to buy it doesn't mean you need it. Stop wanting everything you see. It's time to get focused on your purpose. How long will you stay immature when there is work to be done? The growing process begins with milk, just as the stages of a baby begin with milk as the child grows.

As a growing Christian, there is a time when you must be weaned off milk. God is weaning you off milk, but you prefer to remain a youth. God wants us to grow, so he gives us bread, which is substantial to life. But the word says in Mathew 4:4 - *that man must not live by bread alone.* Meat makes us stronger, giving us the strength to endure. God is maturing you. If you are still on milk, it's time to grow up. What diet are you on?

14

YOUR TEST IS BIRTHING A NEW BEGINNING

Isaiah 43, John 4:24, John 10:27, Psalms 119:71, Romans 8:28, John 5:39,
Proverbs 18:24, Psalms 121:1, Luke 7:47, Ephesians 3:20, Luke 16:8,
Jeremiah 33:3, Proverbs 30:9, I Peter 1:4-9, Matthew 6:33,
I Thessalonians 5:3, I Thessalonians 5:17

Indeed these are the last days; the spirit of *entitlement* is prevalent throughout the Earth. You're living in a time where sanctified, tongue-speaking, Holy Ghost-filled Christians fail to acknowledge God outside of the church. Consulting him *only* when they're in trouble or need a blessing, but this is not God's intention for his church. Instead, believers must reverence him as the only true and living God and continuously commune with him daily. (I Thessalonians 5:17) Don't expect to develop a strong relationship if you neglect to spend quality time with him. *It's time to get to know God.* He's destined you for greatness. Jesus died on the cross for *your sins,* not his.

Therefore, you're indebted to him. Psalms 119:71 *"it was good that I was afflicted,"* implying there is progress and growth through pain. You can't get away with murder anymore. Stop aborting the dreams He's placed in you. God is birthing something new in you, and it's coming through your suffering, don't avoid it – embrace it. Don't allow people to break you down, *"Greater is he that is in you, than he that is in the world."* (1 John 4:4). You can't continue doing the same thing expecting a different result; that's *insanity*. Instead, shift your attention; stop focusing on your storms but reflect on what he's trying to do through you. (Psalms 84:11) Your God wants to *birth greater*.

15

THEN THERE WAS A SOUND

ELDER STACY SIMS

Psalms 34:17-19, Psalms 107:6, Judges 2, Judges 6:6

Israel was a chosen people, set apart and called by God. The Lord delivered Israel from bonds of slavery in Egypt and blessed them with houses they didn't build and vineyards they didn't plant. Somewhere after transitioning from bondage, the Israelites became weary in the process before possessing the promised land. God was looking for the Israelites to be committed, accountable, obedient, and serve no other gods. This expectation is still relevant and applies to the modern church. Believers of God must be accountable, dedicated, and obedient to leadership in order to receive all the promises of God.

The Lord wants to hear a righteous cry from his children so he can bring you out. (Psalms 34:17) There is no wiggle room in holiness. You're either in or out, hot or cold. (Revelation 3:15-16) God is not concerned with your past but your future. He wants you delivered and liberated by his spirit. (II Corinthians 3:17) The best is yet to come, but you must first listen to the voice of the Lord. Now's your opportunity to send up a sincere sound of worship to the father, and he'll come to your rescue.

16

I WANT TO LIVE

Luke 19:1

Church, are you ready to mature in God, moving from milk to meat? Death, sickness, and despair happen suddenly, and the church has to stop playing games. The house of God must be a place of love and peace, where the fruits of the spirit are evident. It is impossible to have true fellowship when envy and jealousy exist. This year, Immanuel has undergone a few adjustments, focusing on lifting and encouraging others to advance from milk to meat. Don't let your self-will cause you to miss the call of God. Continuously demonstrate kindness because life's too short, be wise, and go to one another in love and meekness. The church's objective is to **spread** the gospel, instill **faith** in the hopeless, **and strengthen** the weak. You've been placed on assignment. It's time to get to work. The devil's not playing; exemplify power under control.

17

—————

ARE YOU READY FOR A MIRACLE?

Acts 3:1-10, Luke 10:2, Exodus 20:12, Hebrews 13:17

Church, are you ready for a miracle? Someone's coming out of fear and chaos to make a difference in this generation. Countless world changers haven't accepted God's call in this building. He's giving you an opportunity to make a vow to serve him. The Bible says, *"The harvest is great, but the laborers are few."* (Luke 10:2). God called the church to serve one another in love and minister to the community. Let's put things in perspective. There's greatness in you to fulfill his purpose; instead, the saints are more concerned with the crowd and who doesn't like them. You have the power to break out - shake off fear, depression, and anxiety and put on *faith*. Make a detour and let God make you over again. Are you ready for a miracle?

18

ALMOST DEAD, AGAIN

I'M COMING BACK ALIVE

1ST LADY ELLAZEAN JOHNSON – CO-PASTOR

Ezekiel 37:1-6

Things you will experience in life will shape you and make you who you are—arguments and disappointments that will drain you and circumstances that will try to kill you. But we serve a God that is in the midst of all our trials and tribulations. When our phones lose battery life, we find a power source to restore power. The same should be true of our souls. When the spirit tells you it is dying, you need to plug into the power of Jesus. Get to the altar, and call on his name. Don't just sit in the house of God and die. In Ezekiel 37:3, God asked, *"Can these dry bones live?"* What things have you feeling empty, insufficient, and dead? What is killing you? Is it those hidden sins of past ungodly relationships, lust, alcohol, weed, etc.? The flesh is weak, and self-soothing will not satisfy you. Only God's liberty and freedom in the Holy Ghost will keep you. The enemy can hit us so hard that it feels like a death blow. But it is God's unconditional love that sustains us. Express yourself to God, and ask him to help you. When you mess up, confess up. Come back so you can live.

19

JESUS, THE GRAVE OPENER

I Corinthians 15:1-20

For a single purpose, Jesus came into the world to reconcile humanity back to himself. He didn't die to lavish you with mansions and fancy cars but to save you from this carnal and wicked world. Therefore, the church must get back to the old-time way, where there was more Holy Ghost and less lasciviousness.

So many living among us are dead, not physically but mentally. They are walking and talking but dead in their thinking. God is the *grave opener* and wants to lose those trapped in chains and bondage. This society is hung up on the outer appearance, but God is focused on the inside (the spirit man). Think back to the day he opened up your grave and offered you abundant life. Don't become selfish but introduce somebody to Christ so that he may do away with their chains and give them eternal life.

20

JESUS, THE GRAVE OPENER

Genesis 3:9-13, Philippians 3:12, Psalms 46:1, Proverbs 1:5, Ecclesiastes 5:3, Hosea 4:6, Acts 9:1-10, James 4:6-10, Jeremiah 3:15, Romans 8:1 & 6:11, John 8:36 & 15:7, I Thessalonians 4:11

God expects nothing but the best. He's coming back for a church without a spot, wrinkle, or any such thing. (Ephesians 5:27) As a result, God is giving his church time to get their act together before *the rapture*. To *hide* is to cover, put or keep out of sight; conceal from the view or notice of others. Many believers have sinned and gone into hiding, but the all-knowing and all-seeing God can pull you out of whatever you're in. Submit yourself to his word, and it will bring you out of hiding. (John 15:7) Trust God, for there's a blessing in obedience.

God said to draw nigh unto me; he's calling you out right now. Your opportunity is here, come to the Lord with a willing heart, and he'll turn your life around. Do not disregard the voice of God. Come out of hiding before it's too late.

21

IF THE WRONG THING COMES TO MY HOUSE, IT WILL DIE

CO-PASTOR ELLAZEAN JOHNSON

Judges 2:6-8, Judges 4:1-22, Joshua 24:15, Acts 1:8,
Ecclesiastes 1:9, Galatians 5:1

Joshua, the son of Nun, was a mighty man of Valor. He had many roles: captain over Israel's army, a warrior, a minister, and Moses' protégé. Nevertheless, Joshua was faithful to the Lord and made a vow in Joshua 24:25, *"as for me and my house, we will serve the Lord."*

After the death of Joshua, the children of Israel strayed from God, losing their way. Instead of focusing on God's directive, they began to envy other nations wanting to be like them yet disobeying God. Instead of being set apart (sanctified), they decided to intermingle with the dwellers of the land and serve their gods. Unfortunately, their actions caused them to lose their praise and get out of fellowship with God.

When there's a spirit in the land that's not of God, do not draw towards it because it's not the Lord's will for your life. Lasciviousness and lust are *dominant spirits* in the Earth today but don't allow them to come into your house. God desires you to walk in freedom and liberty, not be entangled in bondage. (Galatians 5:1) Every battle begins in the mind. Free your mind today by pulling down every stronghold incarcerating you; break free. It's time to grow up and fight for your life.

22

LORD, GIVE ME THE STRENGTH TO LIFT MYSELF UP

Luke 13:10-13, Colossians 2:10, Matthew 11:28

Unfortunately, there are more distractions to deal with now than ever before. Folks are immersed with things meaningful to them: food, money, and entertainment. But remember, no one is totally complete without Christ, *"You are complete in him."* (Colossians 2:10) . Many cannot physically pick themselves up like the woman with the infirmity who was bound for 18 years. (Luke 13: 10) Everything changed once she ran into Jesus, who had the power to fix anything.

No matter the problem or circumstance, pattern your life after Jesus and pick yourself up. In the holy word, Jesus never dwelt on the problem but focused on the solution. *What are you focused on today?* You may be walking through the fire, but you're not in it alone. Shift your focus, place all your strength in Christ, and everything else will follow. It's not what it looks like. God is faithful and will never cease to come through for you. He'll do it again!

23

THE COST OF DISCIPLESHIP

*Matthew 4:18-23, 5:16, & 7:13, John 1:5, 6:24, & 7:7, Luke 14:25-31,
Psalms 30:5, I Timothy 4:3, I John 1:7-10, Romans 1:16*

What are you willing to leave to follow Jesus? Generally, people do not like to hear the truth today. But rather listen to things that tickle their ears and boost egos. Folks want to be free but don't desire the truth that results in liberation. This explains why the spirit of deception is so prevalent in this era. When continuously walking in sin and darkness, a numbness will set in. The world is saying to *turn off the lights* so all sorts of ungodly activity can continue without condemnation. This is the church's opportunity to rise up and represent the father in the world. (Matthew 5:16) Unbelievers despise the light of Christ, but God is still strengthening and delivering. There's time to turn things around, confess your sins to the father, repent and go the other way. Church, keep your lights on high beam so that God may get the glory out of your life. The devil is working on every side, but God is greater. Stay on your knees until you get your marching orders, and everything will work together for the good.

24

GUESS WHO'S COMING TO DINNER

Luke 19:1-10, Matthew 24:42, Proverbs 7:8, Philippians 3:10

If Jesus showed up for dinner, what would he see? Would you welcome him with open arms, or would you have to clean the house first? As a sanctified, born-again believer, you must stop living as if God is never coming back for his church. Zacchaeus was a rich, resourceful man, the chief tax collector, who was not popular. Zacchaeus heard Jesus was passing by and wanted to see him, but there was a large crowd. Since he was short in stature, he had to climb up in a sycamore tree to see Jesus passing by.

Jesus looked up and called Zacchaeus down, saying, "salvation is coming to your house."

What has stopped you from pursuing Jesus today? If you want to dwell with him, invite the Lord to reside in your heart and house. When God comes in, he's cleaning up shop; let him take you to a higher level in him. Climb over the hindrances and naysayers to fulfill your destiny through Christ Jesus.

25

HOW DID WE GET HERE?

FROM BURNOUT TO ASHES

Isaiah 61:1-3, Psalm 51, Romans 14:6

We, as Christians, cannot continue to be pacified and not continue the mission of God. Ashes are defined as the residual of what once was and is no more. Are you a better version of yourself than you were yesterday? Are you on course or just getting by as a Christian? Why are so many Christians walking away from their vocation and their calling? Because they have become so overwhelmed by life circumstances that they have even become deceived. They are prideful and lack substance. Who are you really on the inside when no one is watching? How did you get here? When did you leave your purpose and forget that dream you had?

Stop feeding the negative by the words in your mouth. God wants you to be saved and share his message. But joy and deliverance require work. Spend time with God, not just at church. It's time to let nothing separate you from the love of God. There is joy in God. Get back to that special place in him.

26

____

THE MAKING OF A DISCIPLE

Luke 18:1, Acts 1:8, Matthew 28:20, Matthew 16:18, II Corinthians 3:17,
Psalms 37:37, Colossians 2, Philippians 2:13, Ephesians 6:10, I Samuel 15:22

During these perilous times, God is looking for his church *(his disciples)* to go into all the world preaching and teaching, compelling men to come to Christ. (Matthew 28:20) Unfortunately, today's modern church has shifted its focus from *discipleship* to *membership*. Currently, you'll find mega ministries on the rise, 45-minute convenient services, and leaders seeking name recognition instead of lifting Jesus' name. Many pastors and leaders have become preoccupied with establishing a large following versus developing Holy Ghost-filled disciples. God wants everyone to be one of his disciples, to fulfill their godly purpose here on earth. It is time to choose – pick a side; choose to serve the Lord with all your heart or continue being a harlot for the enemy, living beneath God's expectation for you. (Revelation 3:16) God woke you up this morning so you can *get it right*. Reposition yourself from an **uncommitted member** to a **sold-out disciple** for the Lord. Jesus was an *Overcomer,* and he called the church to be *Overcomers* too. Do not continue to walk in the spirit of <u>disobedience;</u> instead, surrender your will to God and watch Him bless you through obedience.

27

THE MAKING OF A DISCIPLE - PART II

GOD IS STILL IN CONTROL

Matthew 5:18, Luke 22:32, Matthew 24:35, Psalms 24:1, John 19:38, Hebrew 13:4, John 17:12-17, John 14:1, I Kings19:1, Luke 18:1

Jesus tasted death for us. Therefore we must live with both *hope and faith.* During this walk, your faith will be challenged, but it's imperative that you stand on his *word.* Always remember that *God is his word,* and he cannot lie. (Numbers 23:19) God is in control, and he's covering you. Despite the hurdles and obstacles in front of you, *stay focused.*

Jezebel told Elijah she was going to kill him, causing his faith to be tried. Finally, the great prophet Elijah became so discouraged that he asked God to take his life. Still, instead, he sent a ministering angel to deliver his word. God covered Elijah the entire time, and the word brought him out. It doesn't matter what you go through down here, God is with you, and you can make it! *My God is still in control!*

PEOPLE THAT REFUSE TO CHANGE

Genesis 4:3-11, Titus 1:2, Hebrews 12:6,
Proverbs 18:24, John 3:16, Proverbs 29:18

In Genesis 4, Cain slew his brother Abel because he offered a pure sacrifice unto the Lord. Therefore, believers need to stay in communication with God, the source. Through prayer, God will reveal his will and desire to you. Generally, when people do not want to change, they fail to accept when they are wrong or at fault.

On this Christian Journey, you must continue to make strides to be more like God, which causes change. When you fail to change, you fail to accept God's will for your life. Ask yourself whether I need to change or not. Are there attitudes and habits that need to be reversed in order to walk into my destiny? Assess your life today and make the necessary changes to go further in God.

29

TURN AWAY THE FOOL IN YOU

Romans 1:16, Proverbs 14:1-35, Isaiah 43:1-66

Christians are afraid to display or reveal their godly relationship with the world. But the Bible declares that we should not be ashamed of the gospel and all he has done. So many have been healed from death's door and seen the hand of God save them from dying in horrendous car crashes. In those cases, "Jesus" is often yelled aloud, but when around family and friends, too many forget who Jesus is. *Are you ashamed of your deliverance and testimony?* God has done more than you give him credit for, and he's demanding this news get shared. You'll get in trouble when you deny God, for His power brought forth deliverance and brought you out of sin.

Don't be a fool, one who knows the truth and yet turns away from it. Most people can identify a fool when they hear one. Fools are those who profess there is no God though he breathed life into their body. For we know that God is above all and through all, and his name must be praised. Therefore, don't be ashamed of your God.

DREAM KILLERS
KEEP ON DREAMING

*Genesis 37:18-20, I Thessalonians 5:20, Solomon 8:6, Proverbs 29:18,
John 4:20, Philippians 4:13, Philippians 4:19*

Many people have dreams, desires, and a sense of purpose concerning life's plan. Joseph, Jacob's favored son, would get visions from the Lord. His brothers described him as a *"dreamer"* by his brothers because he would share those dreams. Unfortunately, this vexed his brothers, leaving them to envy and jealousy. They felt Joseph was trying to be superior, and he was the youngest. They despised Joseph and hated to see him coming. Eventually, they plotted to kill him after sharing one of his dreams. Be careful with who you share your dreams and aspirations. *Jealousy is as cruel as the grave,* and everyone does not have the best intentions for you. **(Solomon 8:6)**

God didn't die on the cross for hate. He died for love. Don't allow people to stereotype or typecast you by placing limitations on your abilities, "you can do all things." **(Philippians 4:13)**. Remember, God is sovereign and has all power; he'll take you higher and higher. So, keep the faith and ***never*** stop dreaming.

31

DON'T BECOME A FOOL

Isaiah 43:1-11 & 60:1, Psalms 23:1, Daniel 12:1-3, Acts 2:8, I Peter 2:9-13, Matthew 5:13-16 & 6:33, II Timothy 1:7-9, Romans 12:1, II Corinthians 4:1-7, Psalms 53:1 & 14:1, Titus 2:11-13, Revelation 12:7-12

Unfortunately, folks are giving up careers, families, and legacies for temporary pleasure (lust of the eye). Christians have fallen victim to the tricks of this world, leaving Christ for temporal worldly possessions. Wake up, church. Do not become blinded by glitter and gold but identity your true purpose in life as an ambassador of Christ. Stop chasing after things but chase after God. He has everything you need. God can give you favor beyond comprehension if you put your trust in him.

What are you fighting for? What's your priority? This nation is lost and confused. It's the responsibility of the church to bring them to Christ. God brought you out of darkness and clothed you with righteousness for his glory, not to resemble the world. Stop allowing the devil to make a fool of you. Live holy for God is holy. *How can God be glorified when the spotlight is on you?* You were called out to WIN; not houses, cars, or status, but to WIN souls for the kingdom. Evaluate your priorities and get back on track to win God's way. *Church, don't be a fool.*

32

DON'T BECOME A FOOL - PART II

*I Samuel 15:1-23, Ephesians 5:1, II Timothy 2 19-20, I Samuel 13:1-23,
Proverbs 16:18, Revelation 20, Isaiah 1:19-20, Psalms 46:1,
Deuteronomy 28, Hebrew 11:24-26, Matthew 18:20*

Unfortunately, this society thinks more highly of itself than it ought to. Folks are caught up with man's opinion yet not thinking of how their Creator views them. So when you say "yes" to God, your praise will take you places, and it's the same praise that'll bring you out.

Stop striving to obtain the favor of man but work diligently to win God's favor. I Samuel 15 displays how King Saul's priorities were not in order. God called him to serve and obey, but he was more concerned about people and not about how God saw his actions. As a result, the spirit of God departed from him, and he no longer had the favors of God. Disobedience will cause your blessings to be cut off and life expectancy shortened. Disobedience is a wicked spirit that comes with other familiar spirits like lying, witchcraft, pride, and stubbornness. The father will forgive, but you must have a changed heart. Wake up, and don't be a fool. Repent and allow God to order your steps.

33

A NOTE TO FATHERS

Psalms 103:13 & 127:3-5, Proverbs 3:11-12, Joshua 1:9,
Ephesians 6:11-18, Proverbs 22:6

Fathering can be compared to the job of a long-distance runner. Fathering is a marathon, a long and often trying journey. You must be disciplined if you hope to sustain and finish successfully. A man ought to live so that everybody knows he is a Christian, and most of all, his family ought to know. The Bible says, *"Train up a child in the way he should go, and when he is old, he will not depart from it."* (Provers 22:6). As you train your child, be sure you go that way yourself. "Just as a father has compassion on his children, so the Lord has compassion on those who fear Him." (Psalm 103:13)

Fathers must be courageous, vigilant, and lead even in the face of adversity. God says, *"Have I not commanded you?"* Be strong and courageous. Do not be terrified; do not be discouraged, for the LORD your God will be with you wherever you go." (Joshua 1:9) Remember to praise and appreciate the extraordinary men in your life.

34

GET OFF YOUR KNEES FIGHTING

Luke 18, Isaiah 54:1, II Corinthians 10:4-6, Malachi 3,
Psalm 144, I Thessalonians 2:2

The enemy will try to attack your mind with depression, anger, and bitterness, robbing you of your strength. But God has not given you a spirit of fear but of love, power, and a sound mind. I Thessalonians 2:2 tells us *not to be shaken in mind or be troubled neither by spirit, words, or letters.* When faced with negative thoughts, your whole demeanor can change but don't entertain those thoughts. Instead, meditate on God's word and how blessed you are. When you are done praying, start fighting; when the enemy hits you and your family, counterpunch with the word of God. If you don't fight, whatever spirit is on you will remain. For our weapons of warfare are not carnal. Don't let the enemy sit you down. Get up with power and start fighting.

LET THEM SLEEP

DON'T ALLOW THE SLEEPERS TO KEEP YOU FROM YOUR MISSION OR GOING FORWARD

Matthew 26:31-42, Matthew 13, John 5:39, Romans 12:1, Psalms 1:1-3

It's a freedom to dream and envision great success; everyone in here at one time or the other has had dreams and desires. Some aspired to become president, lawmakers, and surgeons, but once the issues of life happened, the dreams turned into nightmares. Circumstances have detoured you from obtaining those dreams. This caused you to feel angry and resentful, not where you hoped to be at 30, 40, or 50 years old. Folks have stopped dreaming but settled for less, merely existing, but life is passing by. But all things, *the good, bad, and ugly, will work together for the good*; church, **"Stay Woke."** (Romans 8:28). A number of you can't move forward until you stop saying *"No"* to God. It's holding back so many possibilities. Today's an opportunity to change the course of history, and you're right where he wants you. Trust and believe the enemy has tricks in his bag to deter you, but the mission is greater than the moment. Remember, it is not your will but his will that matters. (Luke 22:42) Walk over the sleepers, don't allow them to hold you back from reaching your destiny, moving forward, and completing the mission.

36

THE BATTLE OF JERICHO

Joshua 6:1-27 & 1:1, II Corinthians 10 & 29:11, Matthew 6:33, I Timothy 6:6, Isaiah 59:19, Malachi 3:16, Jeremiah 43:3, Luke 18:1

Everyone in this world is experiencing some type of battle in their life. The children of Israel had to face a battle in order to obtain the promises God had for them. The Lord will bring his people out to praise him. *Dividends* are rewards to those who praise the Lord. Saints have been fighting but going about it the wrong way. The word says, *"For we wrestle not against flesh and blood."* Stop harboring hatred and bitterness in your heart. Don't remain in an unforgiving state. It's not worth the joy and liberty Christ gave you. The walls will come down with a shout, not with doubt. Your miracle is closer than you realize. The 7th day is nigh. Jump in with praise and tear down those walls through prayer. Remember that your prayers are strong and mighty.

THE BATTLE OF JERICHO - PART II

Joshua 6:20, Jeremiah 29:11, Isaiah 59:19, Luke 18:1, Psalms 47:1, James 4:1-3, Philippians 4:13, Ephesians 4:1, Jude 1:20-21, Daniel 12:3, I Peter 5:7

Walls are designed to separate or divide, keeping those on the outside from coming in. Many never experience all God has because of walls of iniquity and strife. In order to possess his promises, generational walls must be torn completely (flat) down. The children of Israel had to destroy the wall of Jericho in order to possess their promises awaiting on the other side. Get strong, church, if not for you for upcoming generations. Stop trying to defeat the adversary *(heavyweight)* when you're a *featherweight (lightweight)*. Cast your cares and sit upon the Rock, which is Jesus. (I Peter 5:7) Build yourself up in your most holy faith. (Jude 1:20) The church has grown weak and out of shape and needs to return to the spiritual gym *(the altar)*. Strength and endurance come through the word of God.

The enemy has a foothold on many households; instead of shouting, they're singing the blues. Shift your atmosphere and *SHOUT unto the*

Lord! (Psalms 47:1) If you want that *"thing"* to fall, jump into praise and worship. When there's an urgency in your life, a *SHOUT* will bring the walls down immediately. Use your shout to break every chain; walls are coming down because *"It's Your Season."*

38

____

A MESSAGE TO THIS GENERATION

Psalms 127:1-5, Psalms 71:18, I Peter 2:9,
I John 2:15-17, Proverbs 13:22, Psalms 37:25

The Lord wants to establish a covenant with his creation. *Covenant* means a contract or an agreement between God and his people. There are many good things in store for those who trust and surrender to him; he has blessings upon blessings. The world is in a hostile state, with so much killing and calamity, especially in the black community. But the church still believes God's in control, and the blood still works. The debt was paid over 400 years ago when African ancestors fought through slavery, lynching, and abuse for equality and a better way of life. You couldn't begin to comprehend the price that has been paid through blood, sweat, tears, and humiliation. Now it's time you do your part by helping others. People take so much for granted nowadays, but the Lord teaches them how to pray. The devil is steadily deceiving folks through vanity and lust on social media. So wake up, church, fulfill your assignment; trust God and let Him direct your path.

39

THE PROMISE OF GOD THROUGH JESUS CHRIST

Isaiah 65:23-25, Isaiah 40:31 & 46:10, Numbers 23:19, I Corinthians 4:5, Romans 1:17 & 8:28, Matthew 4:4, Jeremiah 1:5, Titus 1:2, Hebrews 11:6

The enemy sends tests and trials to distract you, ultimately reducing your faith in God, but *he's a liar*. Nothing happens in life without God allowing it to happen. Your God cannot lie. He has your back. (Titus 1:2) Don't be deceived. Just because he didn't answer doesn't mean he didn't hear you. (Isaiah 65:23) There's an appointed time for your release (*emancipation*). Prayer will bring down all the strongholds and generational chains the devil had you in. Someone's faith needs a *realignment*; he's waiting on you to give it to him. Stop incarcerating your spirit, release a shout, and praise unto the Lord to bring down those walls. Keep praying until something happens. In order to have great success when coming to God, *"you must first believe that he is."* (Hebrew 11:6). Keep pushing, Saints. Go through until you get through. Trust in God because your Victory is nigh.

40

I HEARD YOU THE FIRST DAY YOU PRAYED

Isaiah 59:1, Isaiah 65:24, Daniel 10:2, Acts 16:23, I Peter 4,
Daniel 5, Jeremiah 33:5, Jeremiah 29:11

Church, God is concerned about you and hears your prayers. The enemy is skillful at placing roadblocks, obstacles, and negative objects in your path to bring discouragement, but the devil is a liar. The father loves you; he's faithful and will never leave or abandon you. His timing is not yours; therefore, he has an appointed time to answer your request and fulfill your needs. Don't cease to pray, praise, and thank God for all he's done. Continue to move forward and trust him because he hears you. Cry out to the Lord, and he will answer in due time.

41

____

GO

*Matthew 28:18-20, II Peter 3:5, Psalms 40:3, Romans 8:28, II Peter 3:9,
Isaiah 6:7-9, Isaiah 43:1-4, I Corinthians 15:10, Acts 9, Hebrews 11:3,
Proverbs 18:10*

The Lord is simply telling the church to *"Go,"* progress forward. He wants his people to have a *"go at it"* mindset. *"Go at"* means attacking, pushing forward, or pursuing. God wants to save this generation and develop ambassadors who are not afraid to go into the world and speak for Christ. But unfortunately, many are preoccupied with personal desires and fail to learn how to fulfill God's purpose.

Often, folks feel they've made it once they have an education, a big car, and a house, but that's not the case. Martin Luther King Jr. said, "No man is free until all men are free." But, realistically speaking, salvation is much more than this. In the day of Noah, there was a great distraction, just like it is now. So many were raised in the church and brought up with Christian values; however, the church is not in them. But it's time to go. The signs of the time are before you. Go, preach to the lost. Speak God's truth to your family, compel them to come not to the church but "come to Christ." God is saying, *Go*, get off the milk, mature, and move forward. God is great and greatly to be praised! LET'S GO!

42

IT MAY TAKE A LITTLE TIME

*Psalms 42:1-11 & 73:2-3, Isaiah 65:24, Daniel 5:1-31, Hebrew 11:1,
Jeremiah 1:5 & 12:5, Matthew 7:5, Romans 8:26, I John 3:22,
I Peter 5:7, I Timothy 6:6, Proverbs 3:5*

The church has become intoxicated, blinded by the things of this world. She's often placing too much attention on what the ungodly are doing instead of focusing on Christ. Jealousy and envy of the wealth of the wicked have caused many to perish. But News Flash: everything belongs to God; all power is in his hands. Why would you trade the creator for his creation? Now's not the time to lose your head. Praise him while you wait. Your praise should not be predicated on position but on the fact that *He will*! Take God off your clock. His time is not your time. In the process, pick up your Bible and worship while you wait. Your strength shall be renewed in patience, and he'll show up no matter the test. You are Victorious. (Isaiah 40:31)

43

LORD, I MISS MY WORSHIP EXPERIENCE WITH YOU

*Psalms 51:1-10, I Peter 2:9, Leviticus 10, Proverbs 3:6,
Isaiah 6, I Timothy 6:6, Philippians 4:13, Ezekiel 3*

Naturally, people desire to be accepted in society but remember, saints, you've been called out, sanctified, and set apart from the crowd. Salvation is a daily walk, but it all comes down to trusting God at the end of the day. If you don't trust him, it will be difficult to serve him with all your heart. Doubt and praise can exist at the same time. Either you're going to worship him or not. There's a war going on inside whether they're going to serve their flesh over their spirit. You shouldn't pursue things that would break down your relationship with God. As the people of God, you must pursue and move forward to a triumph future.

In order to be delivered from ungodly spirits, one must repent and ask God to be set free. Everyone has a testimony of the goodness of God. He's brought you a long way, don't jeopardize progress for a moment of pleasure. Too many have given up on themselves having a pity party while the world is throwing stones. Get up from that low place and rejoice in what is to come. Things are going to get better.

44

WHAT'S GOING ON?

Matthew 24:1, I Timothy 4, II Timothy 2:15, 3:1, II Peter 3:1, John 11

There is a great deception in the church, and it is important to know that Christians can become immune to it. Matthew 24:4-5, Jesus tells us to *"take heed that no man deceive you,"* and many will call themselves Christians but are not. We must be aware of false prophets who try to speak into our lives but are full of lies themselves. It's your responsibility to ensure you do not allow yourself to be deceived. What's happening in the black community, where more black men are incarcerated than at home? As a result, single mothers remain single/unmarried, and the family ultimately cannot grow. Statistics also show that the graduation rate for high school students in the urban area is 89% but slightly higher in suburban areas. With all this going on, we are still full of foolishness. Our attention is focused on what we're wearing, hair, shoes, favorite TV shows, YouTube, Facebook, etc. The enemy wants to keep you distracted while he steals your future. It's time to stop being so selfish and self-centered and consider someone over yourself. Decide today to get rid of those things that will keep you distracted and deceived so you'll know *what's going on.*

45

TURN YOUR NO TO A YES

*Isaiah 6:1-8, Matthew 21:28-32, Isaiah 1:1-31, Philippians 4:13,
Romans 7:24, Romans 2:1-6*

The father has created you to fulfill his will and good pleasure. He painted you in the portrait of life to bring praise and honor to his name on earth. He desires nothing but the best for you. With that in mind, he has empowered and equipped you with the tools needed to fulfill your destiny. Therefore, it's imperative that believers spread the good news of Christ and add souls to the kingdom.

The Lord has called many to serve him and be a witness for him, but sadly, a considerable amount has said *NO*, rejecting his call. But thank God today is a new day. This is your chance to repent and change your *NO* to a *YES*. Time is at hand; tomorrow is not promised; his grace only keeps you. For if not for his grace, there go I. There is still power in the name of Jesus. Call on him, and he'll help you change your *NO* to a *YES*.

46

TO BE CARNALLY MINDED IS DEATH

Romans 8:6, Psalms 27:5, Matthew 6:13, Luke 12:47, Ephesians 6:10-12

Everyone wants to enjoy a better life. Yearning for godly attributes like love, joy, and peace yet fail to surrender their life and will to Christ. Life is a battle full of deceit and wickedness. Many are trying to fight battles carnally when they're spiritual battles. The carnal-minded have no peace, but the Father gives unspeakable joy. Growth and maturity come through God's word.

God desires to beautify you with holiness and endow you with his spirit by salvation. God's people must learn to follow peace with all men and cast their troubles on him. It is better to give folks over to the Lord than completely giving up on them. God is saying, Fret not for *"I Am"* is with you. The Holy Spirit is free and available to those who desire it.

47

YOUR FAITH IS UNDER ATTACK

*Hebrews 11:1, Matthew 6:30 & 8:10, I John 5:4,
I Timothy 6:12, II Timothy 4:7*

If you believe in Jesus Christ, you automatically have an enemy known as Satan by default. You may not realize you're in a spiritual battle -- but you are. The enemy is a strategist; he's constantly plotting against you, trying to distract you. He knows that your life will be scattered and chaotic if he can keep you scatterbrained in your thoughts. But I'm here to inform you that the devil is a liar. Believer, *"you must continue to fight the good fight of faith."* (**I Timothy 6:12**). Anything valuable to you is worth fighting for. It's high time, church. Now is the season to fight for your salvation, your family, and the kingdom of God. The Bible declares, *"we are more than conquerors."* (**Romans 8:37**)

Jude 1:3 says, "earnestly contend for the faith" (FIGHT). God is forewarning you to work on your *FAITH*. Make a change; begin spending more time in the word, and attend Bible Academy regularly. Because *"faith cometh by hearing, and hearing by the word of God."* (**Romans 10:17**)

How bad do you want it? Fight for it!!

48

FINISH THE FIGHT

JOYCE TYUS - ASSISTANT PASTOR

I Samuel 21:15

As an ambassador of Christ, you'll be engaged in a battle. Some have experienced the same giant year after year. At the same time, some have resolved to stop fighting and pressing forward, discouraged, and feeling defeated for all the efforts made thus far. But whether you decide to just stand on the battleground or swing back, you're still in a fight. It's time to make up in your mind whether you're going to exist or be victorious in the battle. News flash, you're not in this battle alone, and quitting can cause a major catastrophe to fellow soldiers, leaving them vulnerable and open to the enemy.

Though you may be weary and worn, lacking the essentials to continue the battle, you still can't quit. As tired and discouraged as you are, you still have to fight. Warriors may suffer battle fatigue and casualties during the battles, but ask God to strengthen you to slay those giants. So arise, church, get in position, and fight for what's yours.

WHY SIT WE HERE UNTIL WE DIE?

ASSISTANT PASTOR CORNELIUS SIMS

II Kings 7:3-9, Romans 8:31-39

To 'sit' is defined as resting the body in a particular place or location, a period of sitting. The saints have become too comfortable sitting day-to-day when work is done. God wants to excel the body of Christ, but we are too busy being lazy and sitting on our gifts and talents. So many things happen to the body with prolonged sitting, such as heart disease, diabetes, weight gain, DVT, etc. But stand and declare the Lord. It's time to get out of that spiritual slump and get moving. The world is changing, and we need to get on point. Sin has weighed you down and hindered your connection with God. But if God be for us, who can be against us. Saints, it's time to get out of ourselves and into God. Where the head goes, everything else will follow. So let's get up and start moving.

50

IT'S A TOUGH JOB, BUT SOMEBODY HAS TO DO IT

WILL YOU BE THE ONE?

ELDER SYBIL BATES - IHP

I Samuel 17:32-37, Romans 8:28, Philippians 1:6 & 4:13, I John 2:14 & 3:8 Matthew 6:33, Genesis 34:7, Proverbs 8:21

No matter how young or old you are, there's some type of giant to fight. Giants can come in the form of depression, past hurt, or anxiety, but God is more than able to slay them. Sex trafficking is proliferating amongst the black community, but the devil is a liar. God's will shall prevail.

Our youth needs to get all of God while in worship service, covering them from the enemy's attacks. God has a work for the youth, and he shall finish what he has started. Know *you can do all things through Christ*. IROCK, seek and receive the Holy Ghost to give you the power and increase your confidence. Stir up the gift, bind generational curses and walk in your purpose, disconnecting from negative folks. You're an unstoppable force. The fight is fixed, so move forward. Giants have to die today. Use the power within you and fight. Will you be the one to slay the giants in your life? Now's the time!

51

THE COST

II Samuel 24:1-25

Some people don't understand the value of things because they don't understand what it means to make a sacrifice in order to have something. They're accustomed to only receiving and never giving. There is nothing wrong with counting our blessings as long as we are not counting them to see if we have enough. God's blessings *make rich and add no sorrow*. Our security is not in our numbers but in our God. Ultimately, it is an act of extreme disrespect for us to think that it costs us too much to repent for our sins since God sacrificed His only Son to pay the cost for our salvation. What cost are you willing to pay to *have life and that more abundantly*?

52

MY POWER SOURCE - WHAT ARE YOU PREPARING FOR?

DON'T MISS YOUR INTERVIEW; DEPENDING ON MY ALTER EGO & TAKING CUTS FROM MYSELF

APOSTLE JEFFREY CARSON – HOUSE OF REFUGE DELIVERANCE MINISTRY

Matthew 4:18-25 & 20:16, Romans 10:14-17, Isaiah 54:17

The church must recognize who's their power source. When you come to God's house, you're going to be interviewed by God. Your thoughts, attitude, personality, and motives are under review. When going on a job interview, a great deal of preparation goes into it —arranging and coordinating your attire, adjusting resumes, preparing responses, displaying professional mannerisms, etc. The goal is to demonstrate attentiveness and competence to ultimately land the new position. Each time you ask God for something, you're under examination. When entering his house, we must come with thanksgiving and praise. (Psalms 100:4)

As Believers, you must rely on your alter ego, the Holy Ghost, to carry you through. Many people want to take cuts in life, but you've got to go through the process, which requires faith. Your alter ego, the Holy Ghost, is your power source. It will keep your record clean and lead you on a victorious path. Be reminded that *"No weapon formed against you shall prosper."* (Isaiah 54:17)

YOUR YESTERDAY WILL NOT DICTATE YOUR TOMORROW

II Chronicles 20:15-17

Jehoshaphat was the king of the tribe of Judah. He had a number of enemies (Ammonites and Moabites) who desired to smite Israel. Once Jehoshaphat learned a great multitude was after him, fear struck him, and he began to seek the Lord. King Jehoshaphat was surprised when the enemy entered his country and declared a fast in all of Judah. He stood among the people and began to call upon the Lord for "help." The spirit of the Lord came in instructing Jehoshaphat to not be afraid or worried by the great multitude but to trust in God, *"for the battle is not yours, but God's."* So God sent His word to Jehoshaphat, saying, *"ye shall not need to fight in this battle: set yourselves, stand ye still and see the salvation of the Lord with you."*

In today's terminology, God said, the victory is yours - don't worry about it, let your praise fight for you!

Later in history, Judah was taken captive for seventy years by Nebuchadnezzar, king of Babylon. The prophet Jeremiah writes to the captives in Babylon to bring hope in the midst of despair. In this day we're living in, we can't afford to go 5 seconds without hope. Jeremiah 29:11-13 states, *"I know my thoughts toward you, thoughts of peace and not of evil."* Now is not the time to repeat the mistakes of your past, but to press forward and obey the word of the Lord, which will lead you to a brighter future.

4 R's: Regret, Repeat (Do not Repeat Past Mistakes), Repent, Restoration

54

IT'S MY TIME

EVEN ON THIS

MINISTER SHERELLE HOGAN–IHP

Mark 5:25, Romans 8:28, I Peter 5:7

Many try to fix issues they're in, not understanding it's God's issue to resolve, give it to him. (I Peter 5:7) The woman with the issue of blood bled for twelve long years. She spent all she had on the matter, only to get worse. After suffering all she had and being sick for so long, the realization set in; she couldn't save herself. She pressed her way through when she heard Jesus passing through despite the crowd and naysayers. She knew it was her time. Immediately after touching the hem of his garment, she was instantly made whole of her infirmity. He can do the same for you, even in your brokenness; come to Jesus because it's your turn. Give God a praise of thanksgiving because it's your turn.

55

ALMOST DEAD, AGAIN - PART II

I'M COMING BACK ALIVE

1ST LADY ELLAZEAN JOHNSON

Ezekiel 37:1-6

Life experiences and tribulations will shape the direction of your life. Disagreements and arguments tend to drain you, resulting in stagnation if you allow it. Remember, God is mighty and in the midst of every situation. It's important to stay connected to your power source. When a cell phone loses battery life, you plug it into the charger to restore power. The same thing is true spiritually. When your soul is dying, you need to tap into Jesus, the number one source.

Ezekiel 37:1-6, God says, *"Can these dry bones live?"*

Ask yourself what things have you feeling empty and dead and what's killing you? The flesh is weak, but self-soothing will not rectify or resolve the issue. Only God's liberty and the Holy Ghost can liberate and make you free. The enemies' goal is to knock you out with a death blow, but God's unconditional love will keep you. So get on your knees and ask God for help. Then, when you mess up, confess up and come back to God so you can live.

PART III

1

MY HELP IS STANDING BY

MY PRAISE IS WHAT I GIVE BACK TO HIM

Psalm 12:1-8, Psalm 50, Psalm 23, Hebrews 11:6, Acts 20, Romans 5

To help means to give or provide what is necessary to accomplish a task or satisfy a need; to aid or assist. Psalm 46 says that God is our refuge and strength, a very present help in trouble. Despite what you are going through, run to Jesus, not other substances such as alcohol or drugs. The Holy Ghost is your help. God can answer all your prayers the way you ask but will respond the way he wants. The key is faith. If the key doesn't fit, it's time to adjust your praise. The devil thinks he has you. But you are coming out with a praise. Get off the ropes, put on your breastplate and come out swinging. With your hands lifted in praise, look to God. He is your help. God is standing by.

2

____

GOD IS STANDING BY - PART II

Psalms 116:1-19, Isiah 43:18, Isaiah 55, Matthew 24:4,
Jeremiah 33:3, Numbers 23:19, Hebrews 5, Malachi 3:10

Regardless of the mountain or test, God is standing by. His word is settled in heaven and does not change. So many are trying to please man and gain their approval when the focus should be placed on God. Hang in there during the season of trouble. Get folks and their opinions off your mind. Rebuke the spirit of fear believing the father in heaven has windows open just for you. This is the season of windows open.

3

TO WORSHIP

Romans 13:1, Psalms 46:10, Romans 5:1, Psalms 23:3-4,
John 10:27, Psalms 34:1, Isaiah 55:8, Luke 18:1

To worship is to reverence God, to kiss him for who he is. Throughout the day, man must learn to worship him and *"be still and know he is God."* (Psalms 46:10). **Hope** is a favorable expectation; while **anxiety** is expecting the worst, things won't get better. Be patient during the process with the realization he's creating something better inside of you. Worship God through tribulation. He hasn't forgotten you; get to know him and recognize his voice. Anyone who hungers for God has access to him, whether rich or poor. Unfortunately, some people disconnect from God as soon as they leave the church. You must take the Lord with you everywhere you go. Too many are standing tall physically but bowed down in the spirit. This year is a great time to throw punches and give the enemy a black eye. Elevate your worship and praise God for who he is.

4

PRAISE & WORSHIP - PART II

John 4:21-24, Ecclesiastes 12, Revelation 22:21, I Kings 17:7-16

"Worship" is a vital part of your Christian walk, the time of intimacy with God. John 4:24 expresses, "God is a spirit: and they that worship him must worship him in spirit and in truth." To be a true worshiper, you must tell the truth. God will judge everything we do, but he won't tolerate a liar. Psalms 101:7 says, "A liar won't tarry on his sight." To obey God, you must be willing to change your position. When you become a worshiper, you give God his first. Every person must willingly give up something they want to get what the father has for them. Genuine worship won't leave you empty, and it's your reasonable service to bless him. Your cabinet won't run dry when you bless God first with your gifts, time, substance, etc. Allow the word to wash you and bring forth change in preparation for your assignment. Know that God loves you and wants to get closer to you. Elevate your worship this year.

5

MY PAIN CHANGED MY NAME

Ruth 1:1-22 & 2:1-2, Isaiah 43:1-7, Deuteronomy 28:1-13, II Corinthians 5:20,
I Corinthians 15:5 8, Philippians 4:8, Amos 8:11, Psalm 119:11,
Job 1:21, Hebrews 12:1-3, Psalms 46:10

God chose you to be a witness for his name's sake, his ambassador. In this humanistic society, too many are focused on their needs, not concerned with rendering unto the Lord. During this journey, you'll experience a season of famine, a lack of something. Famines are brought on by droughts, a lack of water. The church is experiencing a famine because there's a drought of pure worship. (Amos 8:11) Hell is all around but look up. God is with you every step of the way. The devil will mess up your mind if you let him. Please don't lose your peace trying to save someone else; save yourself. It's not quitting time; come too far now, "God will turn all your pain into gain" by changing your name. (Ruth 1:1-22) Saints "continue to go through until you get to"; your pain has a purpose. "If you want a testimony, endure the pain." What your pain is producing is greater than this present discomfort. At the end of the day, "all the pain and sorrow endured will bring forth victory"; hold on, don't leave God over this.

6

MY PAIN CHANGED MY NAME - PART II

Romans 7:13-25, 3:23 8:28 & 10 Ch., Ecclesiastes 12:14, Galatians 5:13, Psalms 119:11 & 119:105, Revelation 2:29, James 1:15

Medical professionals have labeled illnesses like Hypertension the *"silent killer,"* but the number one killer continues to go undetected. Sin is the leading killer of mankind throughout the world. In this humanistic society, many are zombies (walking dead); they're asleep yet numb to what's happening around them. More and more people are drawn away by their own lust and desires, blinded by the fact it's destroying their lives. Once lust has formed, it brings on sin, leading to death.

We must allow God to lead us and order our steps on this walk. Live in freedom and absolute truth. First, be honest with yourself, repent, and ask him to direct thy path. Then, seek God with a pure and loving heart, and choose love over hate. Finally, challenge yourself to maintain the right spirit and attitude throughout your day and watch all things work together for the good.

MY PAIN CHANGED MY NAME - PART III

Ruth 1:20-22, Psalms 122:1, Isaiah 55:1, Psalms 34:8,
Acts 17, Isaiah 4:1, Revelation 2:9, Matthew 11:29

In this day and age, so many people are trying to escape reality through television or social media. Clueless on what to do, running from one situation after the next when they ought to be running to God. Don't sell out for a cheap thrill when God can abundantly bless you in less than 40 seconds. Stop believing God thinks like you but begin to think like him; he has a purpose for you. To have a rich life, you must serve the Lord. Signs of the time tell us these are perilous times. Think yourself happy. Joy must be restored to the house of the Lord. Don't lose your taste buds for Christ.

8

HE FOUGHT THE BATTLE, BUT I WON

Acts Ch. 27 & 28

Acts 27 and 28 detail Apostle Paul's encounter with the storm. Paul, a prisoner of God, was on a ship on the way to Rome when a storm arose. Many were on the ship with him, mostly prisoners, some guilty and others innocent, but they persevered through the rough currents. So many here face various types of storms: discrimination, poverty, sickness, and the like. It doesn't matter how bad the storm is when the right person is on the ship, and Jesus will be with you through it all. While in the storm, change your attitude from despair to hope. It's so easy to forget who you are while in a storm. The uncomfortable experience will produce a testimony. Thou thoughts may come to abandon the ship and give up, hold on to the broken pieces and go forward. For the word said not a soul shall be lost. They looked for Paul to die, but God kept him through it all. When you go forward, the Lord promised that he'd show you his glory; hold on.

9

THERE IS NO OTHER WAY

Genesis 11:1, John 14:2, II Peter 3 Ch., Romans 6:23, Isaiah 6,
Hebrew 11:30, I Corinthians 5:17, I Peter 2:9, Hebrew 1

Jesus is the way, so why are Christians trying to find another way? In Genesis 11, God confused the people after trying to build a tower that reached heaven. Their language was babbled, creating great confusion, then scattered them abroad. You are born for a purpose. This world is confused, the government is confused, and even family and friends are confused, but the one thing that remains constant is *God*. This generation is self-absorbed and narcissistic, but the children of God must stay focused, walking in purpose during these last and evil days. The nation is frantic, unsure of what's to come. But the people of God have to remain vigilant, leaning on his word. So keep your cool, saints, and let your light shine in the midst of this dark nation. Ain't nobody God but God.

10

THERE IS NO OTHER WAY - PART II

Genesis 11:1-8, Isaiah 40:8, John 17:17, Galatians 1:6-9,
Matthew 4:4, Proverbs 30:5-6, Matthew 25:12, I Thessalonians 5:1-4

The church has lost sight of what to do during these times. Many no longer adhere to biblical principles like studying the word or devoting quality time in prayer talking to God. Yet investing more time in carnal matters such as sitting in front of the hella-vision all day. The church is suffering from "reckless endangerment." Don't miss God being stagnant and focused on doing your own thing. Be intentional. Get on your job for the Lord; he's coming like a thief in the night. (I Thessalonians 5:2) Don't be left behind; make preparation for eternal life.

11

FAITH PUT ON TRIAL

James 1:3, Hebrews 11:1

James 1:3 says that knowing this, that the trying of your faith worketh patience. Our faith is being tested, but a faith that can't be tested is a faith that can't help you. Hold on to your faith because it is holding on to you. Now faith is the substance of things hoped for, the evidence of things not seen. (Hebrews 11:1) We hold on to this hope during this unemployment crisis, business shutdown, church and school closures, and trust God. We all have fears to overcome, but don't let those fears overtake you. Be kind to one another, not just during this time but all the time. While you sit at home, release the unforgiveness you feel toward certain people. This disease is bigger than your displeasure for one another. It's time to lay aside judgment and pray. When this is over, don't get cocky and try to outdo one another and party; instead, PRAY and PRAISE. Don't let this shake your faith. There is a purpose in everything. Where is YOUR FAITH?

12

THE COST OF DISCIPLESHIP

Matthew 4:18-23, Luke 14:25, John 4:24, Psalm 119, II Timothy 4

What are you willing to leave to follow Christ? Have you counted the cost of being a Christian and follower of Jesus Christ? As a believer, you will have to make several sacrifices on your daily walk. We live in a world that thrives on deception. And most people can't handle the truth when it's a clear reflection of their character. But Jesus tells us the truth, and the world hates him because of it. And they will hate you too. Christians are being killed every day because of their belief. Now is not the time to turn off the lights. The world is walking in darkness where sin lives, but God is light. Don't let the lust of the flesh, lust of the eyes, and pride of life keep you in darkness. Watching and listening to unclean things can make you do unclean things. Don't be conformed to this world. (Romans 12:2) Stop stumbling when you have the power of God. Don't be weary in well-doing. (Galatians 6:9) Keep marching.

13

MIRACLES

Ezekiel 37, John 10:10, Proverbs 29:18, Psalm 121:1-2

Prayer is essential and has become even more important in these difficult times. Don't give up on God despite what you may be going through because he hasn't given up on you. We are nothing without him. It's time to see beyond now. Proverbs 29:18 says, *"Without a vision, the people perish."* Repent! People are dying, and the vulnerable suffer while our leaders and ministers sit up high in their chairs. After this pandemic, *Will you go back to business as usual? Do you hear the cries of the community? Have you become too comfortable?* It's time to put on your whole garment. We are in a valley. Tragedy is occurring everywhere, but *"look to the hills which comes your help."* (Psalm 121) We are all in the same boat, but there is *hope* in our *suffering.* There is a miracle about to happen. *We need a miracle!*

14

MIRACLES - PART II

John 14:27, Luke 12:16, Mark 8:36, I Thessalonians 5, I John 4:18

Despite what it looks like, God is still a healer, and he has the last word. I know that some of you have lost loved ones, and it is a difficult time, but don't lose hope. To those struggling with past addictions because of the isolation, don't go back to those things that had you bound. You are delivered. I speak peace in your home, a peace that only God can give. (John 14:27) The devil wants your mind bound and back in Egypt, but you will come out of this with your mind free. Tell yourself that I shall live and not die. Fear is torment. Don't let fear predict what you will and will not do. God wants you to live. Love is stronger than the grave. Love cast out fear. (I John 4:18). God is still working miracles. Lord, we need a miracle.

15

OUR GOD IS FAIR IN SPITE OF

Genesis 18:23-33, I Timothy 2:1, Ezekiel 18, Psalm 57,
I Corinthians 15, Genesis 19

When bad things happen in this world, people tend to blame God. Why did God allow these things to happen? The word of God says in Ezekiel 18 that all souls belong to God. The righteous, unrighteous, men, women, and children will die. Sometimes the righteous and children perish prematurely to shield them from the wickedness of this world. But there is a safe place in Jesus. We live in a sin-cursed world and were born in sin. But I know a God who can do exceedingly and abundantly above all we can ask or think. (Ephesians 3:20-21) In such calamity, we thank God for the intercessors who have stepped in to pray, not only for themselves and their families but for their neighbors. Saints don't stop praying and trusting God. Walk by faith, despite the data and statistics. God is still working miracles. Are you ready for a miracle?

16

DO YOU BELIEVE?

Luke 7:7-15, 11:5-13, I John 5:2-3, 3:22, Daniel 12, Matthew 6:33

It is so important that the saints don't stop praying. When you pray, pray the word of God, and believe what you are praying. This is a rough time for everyone, but do you believe God is with you? If he did it before, he will do it again. When things get hard, cast all your cares unto the Lord, and he will give you rest. (Matthew 11:28) If God can't do it, no one can. PRAY - PRAY -PRAY. The more you pray, the more your faith will increase. The word says that the just shall live by faith. (Hebrews 10:38) Keep knocking until you get your miracle.

17

I REMEMBER MOMMA (MOTHER)

A MESSAGE TO MOTHER'S

St. John 19:26, James 5

To all the mothers, I know times get hard even more so now living in the time we are in. But God is faithful. Continue to walk by faith and trust that God will provide. God has a way of blessing us. When I think of a true mother, I see one who; nourishes, provides, comforts, and covers. She is there to talk with you. She finds no fault even when you are wrong. A mother will always be there no matter what. If you have not called your mother in a while, do it today. If you have lost your mother, remember the good times you shared. Our mothers are only here for a short while. Spend time with your mother and redeem the time you lost while you still can.

18

ACTS OF KINDNESS

Romans 10, John 1, Psalm 103, Luke 10, Psalm 41, Romans 12

We have seen the best and the worst in people during this pandemic. It's so easy to find fault. But now is not the time to judge and criticize but to help. This pandemic has touched people of all races, colors, ethnicity, and religion. We are all in the same position. But God has given us victory and peace in the midst of the storm. Thank God for Jesus. We have to go farther because God has truly blessed us. Saints, we have to be kinder. If you have the means, there is a need. Romans 12 tells us to present our body as a living sacrifice. Don't be selfish. We all can use a little kindness. Be a little kinder today.

19

ACTS OF KINDNESS - PART II

John 5:39, II Corinthians 5:17, Romans 8:35-37, Romans 12, Luke 10:25-31, II Peter 2, John 1:1, Genesis 1:1, Isaiah 43:11, Ephesians 4:29

There is so much wickedness, rebellion, and evil in the world today. We, as believers, must believe the word of God. But we must be doers of the word, not only hearers of the word (James 1:22). God wants us to grow in our actions, behaviors, and deeds. When people see you, they should see Jesus. It's time to be more like Christ. Forgive those who have done you wrong, and be nice to those who have not been nice to you. You can't fulfill the will of God being full of yourself. Let your light shine. Don't let this world cause you to be callous and contaminate you with hate and bitterness. The love of God is consistent. Lord, teach us to be kind. Be ye kind.

20

POURING OIL IN THE WOUND

Luke 19:7-8, 18:9, Romans 5, Ephesians 2:1, Philippians 2:4,
Acts 2, Isaiah 55, Psalm 14:1

Many are hurting today. Unfortunately, there will always be sick and hurting people among us. It's time to start the process of healing both mentally and spiritually. Your wounds have defined who you are. But there is restoration for your scars. Those scars are a sign of healing and deliverance. God brought you out. Without him, you can do nothing. God will give you peace. John 14:27 says the peace I give to you, I do not give as the world gives. It's time to stop scratching the scars. Instead, let's use our oil for healing through the word of God and praying kindness over others. Pour your oil on someone who needs to be healed.

21

AMERICA NEEDS OIL POURED INTO ITS WOUNDS

Luke 10:25-37, Psalm 18, Ezekiel 36:23, Hosea 4:6, John 14

Oil was used for many things, including healing. Certain ointments were used to treat open and closed wounds. America has a deep wound. But God wants to heal those wounds. God is calling the church to help someone get delivered. It's time to focus on souls and not goals. The church's job is to witness and be a light in this world. The world is sick, along with its leaders. Proverbs 14:34 says righteousness exalts a nation, but sin is a reproach to any people. God gave you a gift, and you will never fulfill it only by thinking of yourself. Ask yourself, *"Why am I here?"* What are you going to do in this season God gave you? It's time for healing.

22

—————

WHAT IF THIS WAS THE END? JUST SAYING!

Isaiah 1:3-19, Daniel 12:1-4, Matthew 5:13-14, 13:36-43

Just take a minute and pause for a second. If this was the end, what would you be doing, what would you be known for? Would you be gossiping or getting your hair done? The church is singing and praising, but their heart isn't in it. Christians do whatever they want throughout the week and then come to church trying to praise God. The preachers have talked enough. The world does not care what God wants. Has the church stopped caring what God wants? If this is the case, we are in trouble. The word tells us in Galatians 6:7 to be not deceived; God is not mocked: for whatsoever a man soweth that shall he also reap. What if this was the end? What frame of mind would God find YOU in? Learn to do well, and ask God to order your steps. God is the only way. Just saying!

23

DON'T LET THEM FORGET MY NAME

Malachi 3:16, Revelations 12, Acts 4:12, Ephesians 2

America, the church, and even the world have forgotten the Lord's name. God's name is associated with his will. It's not America's will but God's will. Matthew 6:10 says *thy will be done.* What has happened to the church? Our job is to go all over the world and preach the gospel. But most have forgotten the name of the Lord because the church has not spoken his name. Many black Americans have lost their lives unjustly. We say their names at home, on social media, and protest in hopes others don't forget them. But how many have forgotten Jesus' name. Let's stop talking about each other and talk about Jesus. Why do we try so hard not to offend others but find it easy to offend God? We are not like the world and need to stop trying to be like it. We represent the name of Jesus. Stay close to God, and speak his name. Remember his name. Don't forget his name.

24

STAY FOCUSED AND STAY ENCOURAGED

Luke 14, Psalm 117:20, Acts 4:12, John 3

God saved us with a purpose. Romans 8:28 says, *all things work together for the good to them who love God, to them who are called according to his purpose.* Purpose is the original intent. What is your purpose? We have become too relaxed. It's time to return to the fire of Pentecost. The church is trying to gain acceptance from the world. But 1 John 2:15-19 tells us that we should not love this world or the things in it. We are so focused on material things, jobs, and personal gain that we forget God gives us something greater: joy, peace, and his word. The church needs some fire, the Holy Ghost, and power. America needs a revival, but they won't get it unless it comes out of the church.

25

DON'T FORGET HIS NAME OR HIS BENEFITS

Psalm 103:1, Isaiah 53

We mustn't take our eyes off of God. Now is not the time to party but a time to put on the whole armor of God, the breastplate of righteousness, and the helmet of salvation. (Ephesians 6:11-20) God is breaking up some stuff so he can water and fertilize you to help you grow. Whatever you need, God's got It. God has healing and blessings with your name on it. But we have to do better. Make yourself available to God, and don't forget him. The word says in Psalm 34:1, I will bless the Lord at all times. Don't forget all the things God has done and all his benefits.

26

REJECTION IS NECESSARY FOR YOUR PROJECTION

Isaiah 53, Jeremiah 12:5

The Bible tells us in Jeremiah 12:5 that if we can't contend with footmen, how can we contend with the horseman. It's so important that we are not caught up with recognition from others. But what God thinks genuinely matters. You can't stay in a place of depression and rejection too long. It's time to get up and shake yourself. Move forward. Tell God that you trust him and keep marching. 1 Corinthians 15:58 tells us to be steadfast, immovable, always abounding in the work of the Lord, knowing that your labor is not in vain in the Lord. No weapon formed against you shall prosper. (Isaiah 54:17). There is healing in the oil. If God can't help us, we can't be saved.

27

YOUR PRAISE WILL CHANGE THE ATMOSPHERE

II Chronicle 20:17-25, Acts 16:25-26, I Peter 2:9,
Psalms 127:1-2, I Corinthians 5:7, Hebrews 13:17

Praise is an expression of admiration, to commend or glorify God. When you welcome the praises of God, your atmosphere will instantly change for the better. Israel and King Jehoshaphat were about to encounter a great attack from the enemy. The King knew his army was no match for his enemies, who joined forces to destroy them. But the Lord spoke, saying, fear not, the Lord will be with you. So King Jehoshaphat and all the inhabitants of the land sent up praises worshipping the Lord. When the singers went forth, the beauty of praise went out before the army. The atmosphere was set, and they were ready for a miraculous move of God. The Lord then set ambushments against the enemy, utterly destroying all their enemies. Invite the Lord in your heart that he may change your tone and shift the atmosphere.

28

YOU BETTER THINK, WHAT ARE YOU'RE ABOUT TO DO TO YOURSELF

Proverbs 14:23, Ezekiel 38, Romans 6:23, John 10

Sin is a transgression against divine law. It sends a reproach and brings shame to you, your family, the community, the church, etc. Sin has nothing to give but death. Romans 6:23 says the wages of sin is death. The church can't continue to fellowship just to say they had a good time. But cast those spirits with fasting and praying. You have more power than you think you have. You just have to plug up to the power source. God wants to give you life and that more abundantly. But the devil wants to destroy your relationship with Christ. Stop playing with the devil because he is not playing with you. Put on your garment of praise and tap into your power source, Jesus.

29

WE CAME TO JESUS AS WE WERE, BUT THE HOLY SPIRIT WON'T ALLOW US TO STAY AS WE WERE

Romans 5:17, 8:23-29, Romans 2, John 14: 26-27, 15:1,
Ephesians 5:26, Galatians 5:22-23

Any man, woman, boy, or girl who confesses to a relationship with Christ and has his spirit is a *new creature*. When God's spirit is received, a transformation begins. After the conversion, you need the Comforter, the *Holy Ghost*. The body of Christ must be the first partakers in fulfilling God's will. Say to yourself, *"God is creating a new thing in me."* Many want to feel his spirit but have a problem hearing the truth. The enemy doesn't want you to know the truth, for the truth will make you free. (John 8:32) *James 1:22 says, "But be doers of the word, and not hearers only, deceiving your own selves.* The spirit is constantly warring with the flesh. Those who continue doing the same things will remain the same. When we accept God's spirit, we become more like him. When you embrace the truth, transformation can occur. Stop fighting against the truth and let God finish the work he began in you. (Philippians 1:6) *"Stay in God if you want to grow in God."*

30

GOD IS TAKING YOU THROUGH A METAMORPHOSIS

Hebrews 12, I John 5, John 15:1, Romans 14:17,
Ephesians 3:20, II Corinthians 5:17

There are four stages in the life cycle of a butterfly: an egg, larvae, pupa, and an adult. In each stage, a change must occur. When we are serving God, we develop and start from point A. God is taking you through a metamorphosis. But there is a process of becoming what God wants you to be. First, don't spend your energy on people who have no desire to change. Secondly, stop trying to appease people and obtain things to prove something. Finally, get your self-esteem in check. God did not die just for you to have things. *God came to give you life and that more abundantly.* (Ephesians 3:20) God knows your thoughts; just please him. It's time to get off milk and go through the entire stage of growth. (Romans 14:17) What stage are you in? Let God continue to develop and help you grow in him.

31

THE MAKING OF A DISCIPLE

Matthew 48:14, John 1:35, Psalm 116, II Corinthians 6:13, Luke 15, I Samuel 3

God said that I will make you fishers of men. (Matthew 4:19) But you have to be patient to be a fisherman. So likewise, you have to be patient to be a disciple. A disciple has an impact on someone; a follower of Jesus; one who convinces others to follow Christ. Oftentimes, we as Christians refuse to leave certain things to follow Christ. We are like a car with the motor running but going nowhere. Thoughts without actions will keep you where you are. You will never be happy trying to be like others. Will you make a good disciple? The one who woke you up needs you. God needs you. Just because you say "No" doesn't change God's agenda. He needs you to be persistent and committed as a man commits to his new bride. You may lose some things when you walk with Jesus but march on.

GOD IS TAKING YOU OUT OF YOUR PIT

Genesis 37:20, Psalm 57:6, Proverbs 26:27, Hosea 3:6, Jeremiah 3:15, Revelations 20:1

A pit is an extremely unpleasant, boring, and depressed place; a deep hole. Unfortunately, there are pits that people dig for us. And sometimes, we dig our own pits like low self-esteem, poor self-image, bitterness, and resentment. Are you holding yourself back by reliving old episodes of your life and believing what others think? Do you always believe the negative? It's time to think yourself happy. Stop telling your sad stories when God gave you a purpose, vision, and dream. Don't let people define who you are. Those trials, hurts, and pains are designed to hold you down. But they are just temporary experiences necessary for your growth. This is just a pit stop.

33

LORD, HELP ME CHANGE THE ATMOSPHERE

Psalm 40:1-8, James 1

Psalms 40:1 states I waited patiently for the Lord; and he inclined unto me, and heard my cry. There are things you go through that will prepare you for what happens next. Some of you are destined for greatness, while others have become comfortable being less than. You will never get anywhere crawling like a worm and feeling sorry for yourself. God wants to do exceedingly more for you. (Ephesians 3:20) So don't give up. Your struggle will bring your miracle. Don't stop praying, praising, and worshipping because it will draw Jesus to you. God won't allow you to stay in a horrible situation. He heard your cry and is going to stabilize you.

34

SHAKE IT OFF

Acts 28, II Corinthians 11, Philippians 4:13, Romans 8:28

Whatever is trying to bind you, *shake it off*! The enemy wants us to live in darkness. But God brought us out of darkness into his marvelous light. (1 Peter 2:9) The enemy has latched on to you because your prayers and life was changing people. We must pray until our light gets brighter. We don't want to live a life where our light is dim and flickering. God, please don't let the light go out. I shall not die, but I shall live because there is still purpose in me. The world won't get better until the church gets brighter.

35

GOD IS PREPARING YOU

Psalm 51, Matthew 24:44, 25:1, Deuteronomy 28:13

Preparation is defined as the action or process of making something ready or the anticipation of something happening. We should be making preparations for the Lord's coming. It is vital that we are prepared for the inevitable, those hiccups that may occur in our lives. Identify the stressors in your life, those things that try to make you mad and take you out of your character. God is trying to tell you to prepare for what's to come. Stop spending every dime you have on sales and the clearance rack. The lord will make you the head and not the tail; you shall be above only and not be beneath. (Deuteronomy 28:13) The enemy is trying to tear you down. It's time to build. There is power in being prepared.

FOR SUCH A TIME AS THIS

Esther 4:12-14, Deuteronomy 28, John 17

Esther was chosen to be queen out of several women. Though she was a Jew, she stood out. God will place you in the front of the bus when the world tries to place you in the back. In the story of Esther, Haman did not like Mordecai because he did not bow to him. There will be people who won't like you because you won't bow to their way of thinking. Stay true to your integrity. Don't become envious of the things in this world. Esther never thought she would be queen and save a nation. God has positioned you for his glory. He has strategically placed you so you can help someone else. Stop being ashamed of the one who saved you. God is shaking the heavens to wake up the world. God is depending on us to declare to this generation for such a time as this.

37

YOU'VE BEEN WEARING THE SAME UNDERGARMENTS FOR TOO LONG

Psalm 66:1-4, Isaiah 60:1-5, 61:1-3, Isaiah 26:3

Some of you appear clean on the outside but are wearing dirty underclothes. Christians oftentimes wear garments of depression and melancholy. They tend to change their garments to that of the world - forgetting where God brought them from. Don't change your position in God. The enemy will pressure you and hit you with everything he has to change your testimony. Stay focused and stay encouraged. Is God losing you to the lust of the flesh, the lust of the eye, and the pride of life? (I John 2:16) He doesn't know you because you changed your garment. God's word will give you what you need to change your garments. Change your garment now while you have a chance. "Lord, help me change my garment."

38

OUR ASSIGNMENT TODAY IS TO PRAISE THE LORD

Psalm 118:19-26, Romans 14:6-9, 8:1, 12:1, I Peter 2:9

God made this day for us to praise him. This is the day that the Lord has made. I will rejoice and be glad in it. (Psalm 118:24) It doesn't take long for God to do anything. It's your faith that is slowing down your miracle. You are settling for what the enemy is feeding your carnal mind. But it is only what God tells you that matters. Whatever he is telling you to do, Do it! Don't worry about the naysayers. God has deposited in your oh just have to believe. There will be hindrances that will try to prevent you from doing the will of God. But remember, we serve a mighty God. He is our savior, and deliverer, and he redeems us to praise him. Our assignment is to praise God today and every day. What assignment are you on today?

39

RELATIONSHIP

I Samuel 18, Phil 2:4-5, Romans 8

God's timing is not our timing. If God says it will happen, then it will; if God says no, it will not happen. Don't let your relationships be diminished because of your will and ego. Our relationships should be based on a firm foundation so our desires do not destroy them. But our relationships will be challenged and tested. Most relationships require trust, the belief that you have the other person's support, and confidence that the other party won't harm you deliberately. Next is vulnerability.

Vulnerability is not a sign of weakness but exposure. If you are going to be in a relationship, you have to be willing to expose yourself. When you have a relationship with God, you sign up for the job. We made a vow, and it's our job to keep it. We can make new friends and get another wife or husband. You can't get another God.

40

THE POWER OF A PAINFUL PRAISE

AP JOYCE TYUS

Psalm 142:1, Psalm 34:1, Luke 4

When others see you praising God, it does not mean you are not experiencing pain or facing trouble. Unfortunately, you don't have to find trouble; it knows who you are and where to find you. Regardless of the pain that Jesus endured, he was faithful to his purpose. Don't let what you are facing devour you. You may be in pain, but you have a purpose. John 10:10 tells us that he came to give us life and that more abundantly. He bought you out for a reason. You are a chosen generation, a royal priesthood. (I Peter 2:9). You have a purpose, and you were created to give him praise. Stay true to what you were created to do. God hasn't stopped being God just because you are going through. Learn to praise God in the wilderness. I will-I will bless the Lord at all times.

41

SUCH THINGS

AP JOYCE TYUS

Ephesians 5:1-4, 22, James 1:22, Revelations 10, Hebrews 5:13, Matthew 25

"*Such*" Is defined as being not specific, similarly, or having the same type or sort; anything with a spot, wrinkle, or blemish. Such things can make you undesirable or unattractive. Such things can leave you with no oil in your lamp. As the body of Christ, we have become "picky eaters." We only want to eat what tastes good. We only want to digest those coming out messages, but we are spiritually bankrupt and lack power. Picky eaters can be categorized as having an eating disorder, but spiritually you have *HOD - Hearers Only Disorder*. But God has a remedy for this disorder. Everything you hear across the pulpit will not always taste good, but it is good for you. Some saints are malnourished and don't have the strength to slay their giants. God's word will never go stale. God is our daily bread. We must hide the word in our hearts to deal with such things.

42

IT'S TIME TO PRAISE THE LORD

Psalms 34:1, James 1:22, Revelations 10, Hebrews 5:13, Matthew 25

It's high time, people of God, to awake out of our sleep. There is calamity all around, trouble on every hand. We, the children of God, must take heed to the word of the Lord like never before. The pandemic is on the rise, and not a day goes by without killing or shooting in our communities, but you were spared for a reason.

Now is the time to draw nigh to God, grab hold of his word and share the good news. Be a daily praise for him, let your light shine, and give him what's due. Let everything that hath breath praise the Lord.

43

LINE UP WITH THE WILL OF GOD

I John 2:15, John 7:17, Jeremiah 17:9, Proverbs 19:21, 14:12, 28:26

It's time to line up with the will of God. When you line up with the will of God, you are able to hear a word. The word is the daily bread that gives us strength. There are too many false prophets not taking heed to what God told them. So don't let your feeling get you jacked up. When you lean on your own feelings and opinions, you are prone to be led astray. Don't stay disconnected from the body of Christ. The enemy will use what your say against you. In your walk with Christ, you must be willing to receive instructions. If you are going to do God's will, you have to dissect and digest the word? God's word never changes. Get in line with God. The Holy Ghost lines up with you when you line up with God. Line up and make plans for God.

44

PUT ON THE GARMENT OF PRAISE

AP STACY SIMS

Acts 16:25-26, Jeremiah 23, John 9, Daniel 3, John 8

Why do we feed the devil throughout the week but shoo him away on Sunday? Are you living like an alley cat? You have to ask yourself if your walk with Christ is worth fighting for. It's not always going to be sunny days. Being saved will cost you something. But the word tells us if we make a vow to the Lord, we should not take it back. (Deuteronomy 23:21) You have to commit to this relationship with God. This generation needs true deliverance but has become suspicious of believers and those who are not committed to what they preach. God has been too good not to allow your light to shine. Meditate on his word daily. Keep living holy. Whatever you are in, you are coming out if God is in it. Don't lose your shout. The world needs to see joy in this dark hour. Use me, Lord!

45

THERE IS NONE LIKE HIM & THIS IS WHY WE GIVE HIM PRAISE

Acts 2:1-4, Matthew 17:1-7, Acts 16

We live in a humanistic, carnal, and secular society where people want to praise God in their own way. There are many religious beliefs, but none other is greater than Jesus Christ. The spirit of influence is everywhere, similar to the spirit of Nero in the Bible days. Unconditionally many Christians believe everything they see and hear, running off emotions and not facts. We serve a God who's brought us out of darkness and loves unconditionally; he deserves your praise. Folks will praise any and everything but don't want to worship God. The spirit of confusion is upon us, but it's time to touch and agree. The book of Revelations is materializing, and time is winding up. At the end of the day, every knee will bow & every tongue shall confess that Jesus is Lord. (Philippians 2:10-11) When God gives you an assignment, and there's no bridge... He will be your bridge. Continue to put on the garment of praise. The Holy Ghost will keep you through it all. Let not your heart be troubled, neither let it be afraid. (John 14:27) Don't let your praise stop, even in this!

46

LORD, DO ME A FAVOR

Psalm 44:1-3, I John 4

When you ask someone to do you a favor, you don't have the time or the resources, and the other person does. And favors are given because you have a relationship but don't forget that favors are returned. Ask God, "Lord, I don't forget favors, but shake me up if I have forgotten any favors." Do you have favor with God? Do you need a favor from him? Stop calling on others who can't do you a favor and call on Jesus. He is on the mainline tell him what you want. Just call him up. Because you have favor with God, you can command those things to leave. You don't have to beg God; just praise him. Find your praise and push out the negative. Live on the favors of God. Lord, I need a favor.

47

DON'T GET BLOWN AWAY IN THIS STORM

Acts 27:1-7, 12-15, Proverbs 18:10, Ephesians 4:13-14, Isaiah 55

A storm is defined as a violent disturbance in the atmosphere with strong winds, rain, lightning, thunder, or snow. We are going to run into storms when we fail to compromise. We live in a different time, a time that we have never seen before. But God chose you to live in this season. Meteorologists can predict storms but not the damages or casualties that come with those storms. Some Christians take warnings too lightly because they feel in control. But no one is in control of God. You can't shake faith. Stay in prayer; whatever comes your way, you will be prepared. The storm isn't coming; it is already here. But it is by God's grace we are not consumed. It's praying time. Don't continue on the same course. Jesus is your foundation. Don't let this storm blow you away.

48

JESUS IS THE REASON FOR THE SEASON

Isaiah 9:6, Luke 2:9-14, Matthew 2:1-23, James 4:8

This year has been full of unprecedented events, but God has been with us through it all. So many have contracted COVID-19, and millions of others have lost their lives to the deadly virus. Through months of pain and heartache, God kept you here for a reason. Pray and intercede for the hurting, the sick, and the bereaved. Numerous families had empty seats at the dinner table this Christmas. Reflect on God's goodness and get busy doing the father's work. Tomorrow is not promised, don't drag your feet but get in line with the word. 'Tis by his grace and mercy that we are consumed. During the holiday time, remember Jesus is the reason for the season. Be thankful for where you are and for what he's done. It's not about things but relationships. "Draw nigh to God, and he'll draw nigh to you." (James 4:8)

ABOUT THE AUTHOR

Bishop Thomas Lee Johnson, Sr. is a man after God's own heart. He is dedicated to the work of the lord, knowing that his life is not his own. Therefore, he has submitted to the will and work of our most high God. Bishop is a native of Detroit, MI, where he was educated in the Detroit Public School system. He is a graduate of Chadsey High School (1965).

Later in life, he was inspired to further his education at Marygrove College. He also holds an honorary (DD) Doctor of Divinity degree from the Detroit Urban Bible College. Bishop Johnson met Jesus Christ on his personal road of Damascus in 1970 and received the baptism of the Holy Spirit shortly after. After faithfully serving under the leadership of his pastor, he was ordained as an elder in 1974. In 1975, he yielded to the call of God and established Immanuel House of Prayer Church. In 1994, he was found worthy of being elevated and ordained as a Bishop. Again, following the leading of the Lord in 2010.

Bishop Johnson established Immanuel House of Prayer-South (IHOPS), located in Darien, GA. Bishop Johnson has a heart for imparting and training upcoming pastors, which led him to establish the Immanuel Ecumenical Council of Churches Inc (IECC). IECC's goal is to witness a coming together of people who share the same common objective of becoming one unified body in Jesus Christ with a heart to fulfill the mission of Christ.

IECC promotes and endorses Apostolic teachings in doctrine, Ecumenical in fellowship, and supports a vision that transcends denominational barriers, religious prejudice, and other spiritual biases. In addition, Bishop Johnson is also the founder of F.A.C.E (Family and Community Enrichment) - a non-profit organization that supports community enrichment and promotes academic growth and development within the urban community.

It is apparent that this man of God carries an apostolic mantel as he is a highly sought-after evangelist, teacher, and anointed preacher. His ultimate desire is for all to experience the love of God, come to repentance, live an abundant life, and possess the promises of God. He is a beloved and courageous pastor determined to lead and love God's people, God's way. A man of valor who exemplifies holiness. The anointing that flows on Bishop Johnson's life is undeniable and has impacted many. Bishop Johnson is a spiritual General in the Lord's army, for he is determined to keep fighting the good fight of faith.